Five Centuries of

Music in
Venice

For
Sir Ashley and Lady Clarke
from H.C.R.L. and J.J.N.

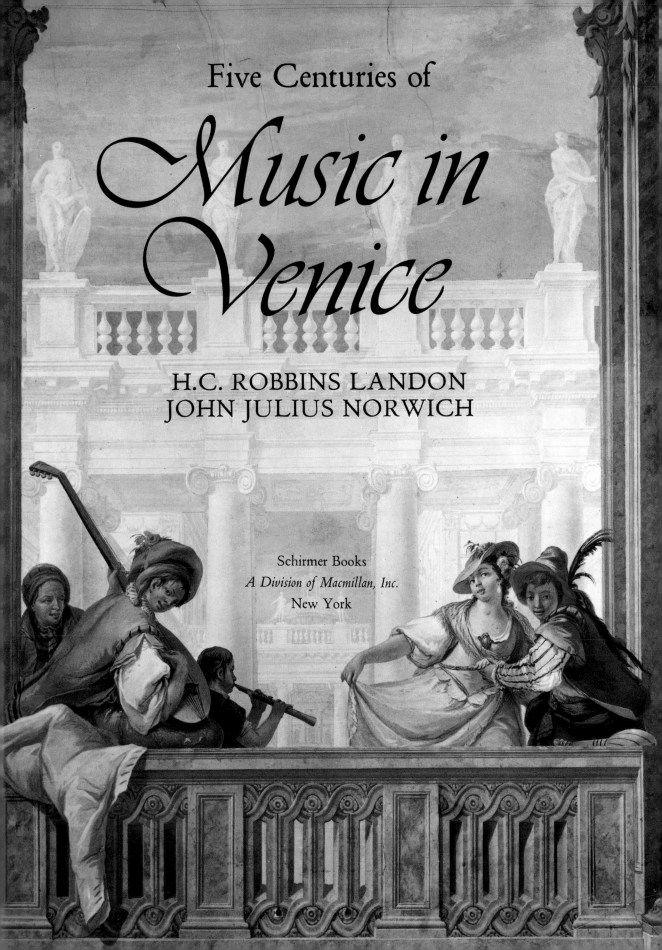

Five Centuries of

Music in Venice

H.C. ROBBINS LANDON
JOHN JULIUS NORWICH

Schirmer Books
A Division of Macmillan, Inc.
New York

COLOR ILLUSTRATIONS

1 *Rich, sonorous, majestic, the brass instruments played by Carpaccio's musicians in his painting of* St George *baptizing the* King and Queen of Libya *are almost audible to the spectator.*

2 *The point where the Grand Canal begins, with the Dogana (Customs House), built in 1625, on the left and Santa Maria della Salute to the right.*

3 *S. Giorgio Maggiore, the monastery island, its church designed by Palladio in 1566.*

First American edition published in 1991 by

Schirmer Books
A Division of Macmillan, Inc.
866 Third Avenue, New York, NY 10022

Collier Macmillan Canada, Inc.
1200 Eglinton Avenue East, Suite 200
Don Mills, Ontario M3C 3N1

First published in Great Britain by Thames and Hudson Ltd., London
Library of Congress Catalog Card Number: 90-49095
Printing number
1 2 3 4 5 6 7 8 9 10

Library of Congress Cataloging-in-Publication Data

Landon, H. C. Robbins (Howard Chandler Robbins), 1928–
    Five centuries of music in Venice / H.C. Robbins Landon and John
Julius Norwich.
        p. cm.
    Includes index and discography.
    ISBN 0-02-871318-4 : $29.95
    1. Music—Italy—Venice—History and criticism.   I. Norwich, John
Julius, 1929–   . II. Title.
ML290.8.V26L3   1991
780'.945'31—dc20
                                                    90-49095
                                                    CIP
                                                    MN

Printed and bound in Great Britain

Contents

Every view of the mouth of the Grand Canal is dominated by the great church of Santa Maria della Salute, designed by Baldassare Longhena in 1630 and finished in 1687. The dome is buttressed by a ring of huge scrolls surmounted by statues.

Preface

First thoughts about the television film that gave birth to this book go back five years, to a meeting in France between myself, my wife and Tony Sutcliffe. During those five years the idea grew and matured. Tony Sutcliffe's wife Jillian Robinson became part of our team. In the Autumn of 1989 we began to write the actual scripts, and I insisted that wherever possible the Directors (Hilary Boulding, John Michael Phillips, Tony Sutcliffe, and Christopher Swann) should come out and work with me.

It was then decided to invite John Julius Norwich to present the film. He soon became involved in all its aspects, so that not only does the TV series owe him an immeasurable debt for having shared his knowledge, his wit and his humanity with us, but so also does this book. It was decided to turn the series into a full-length book. Lord Norwich read the entire typescript and added not only the introduction but also a series of historical and social vignettes as well.

In preparing the original scripts I was greatly assisted by Katrina Cary, who lives in Paris and came down to help me assemble the preliminary material. My wife, Else Radant, also read everything in all its various stages and contributed her usual share of historical perspicacity. When the time came to make a book out of the scripts, I found myself two assistants, both of whom turned out to have remarkable literary capacities; Rachel Cowell and Lucinda Sparke. If the reader finds the text to flow smoothly it is in large part due to the expert editorial assistance which I received.

This book, and the TV series, owe their existence to the Venice in Peril Fund, and part of the income derived from the TV series and the book will be fed to that extraordinary operation, the existence of which is the result of tireless and selfless work on the part of Sir Ashley and Lady Clarke, to whom this book is respectfully and affectionately dedicated by Lord Norwich and myself.

H.C.R.L.

Introduction

One of the most astonishing – and occasionally, it must be said, the most irritating – aspects of the people of Venice down the ages has been their ability to turn their hand to virtually anything, and then to do it quite superbly well. As seamen, they were already in demand by the 6th century, after which their ships dominated the Mediterranean and beyond for the better part of a thousand years. As merchants, they were regularly trading with Russia, Central Asia, India, Siam and China at a date when such regions were, to the rest of western Europe, little more than fable and legend. As imperialists, they administered their own trading colonies in Dalmatia, Greece, the Aegean, the Black Sea and the Levant, to say nothing of a later land Empire that extended westward across North Italy almost as far as Milan. As political theorists, they developed an utterly individual system of government which, though technically an oligarchy, was in fact a good deal more democratic than any other in Europe – with the arguable exception of Switzerland – and which effortlessly maintained itself, with only the minimum of fine tuning, for the lifetime of their Republic. As international statesmen, they were the inventors of modern diplomacy. As industrialists, they initiated mass production half a millennium before Henry Ford.

So much for the more practical side of life. Where the visual arts are concerned, Venice's record is if anything more dazzling still. First, and most peculiarly her own, comes that which stems directly from her Byzantine past: the art of mosaic. In all Italy, her only rival is Ravenna, whose masterpieces date from the middle of the 5th to the middle of the 6th centuries – a period during which, in the words of the Praetorian Prefect of that city, Cassiodorus, the Venetians still lived 'like sea birds, with their homes dispersed, like the Cyclades, across the surface of the water, and secured only by osier and wattle against the wildness of the sea'. But whereas the mosaics of Ravenna, glorious as they are, span little more than a hundred years, those of Venice – in the Basilica of San Marco and on the islands of Murano and Torcello – extend from the 11th century to the 19th. (A good deal too long in fact, since from the 15th century onward the art goes into a tragic decline.)

In painting, the great names crowd in upon us, almost too many to be counted. They are there already in the Gothic days of the 14th century – days before the average man could boast a surname of his own – with Paolo Veneziano and his even more brilliant pupil Lorenzo, breaking the bonds of Byzantine iconography and already clearly pointing the direction in which Venetian art was to evolve. We must also include the Paduan Guariento, whose tremendous fresco in the Sala del Maggior Consiglio of the Doge's Palace, destroyed in the

Water is the Venetian's natural element. In this 17th century painting the expanse of water in front of the Riva degli Schiavoni is filled with boats of all sizes. Those in the foreground are sea-going sailing vessels; in the centre is a row of oared galleys; on either side are hosts of gondolas rowed by one or two men standing in the stern or the middle. BELOW an early aerial view of Venice, published in 1572. The great Baroque landmarks are of course missing, but the general aspect of the city is very much as it is today.

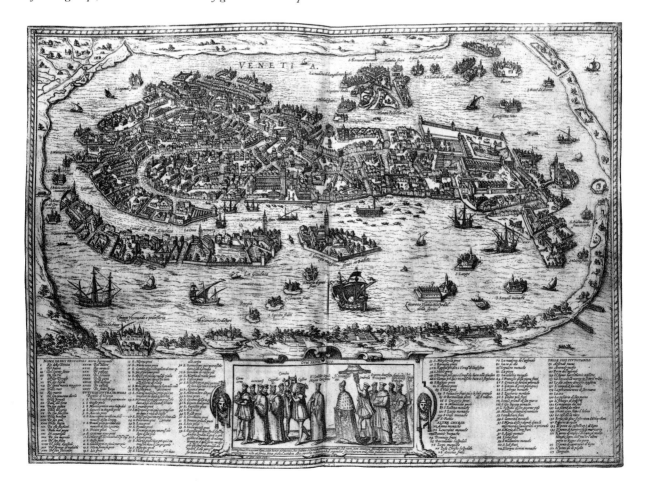

Venice was famous, or infamous, for its prostitutes. Many travellers commented on their numbers and the professional way in which their business was organized. As early as 1500, Carpaccio represented two of them sitting on a balcony waiting for clients.

great fire of 1577, was probably the greatest single artistic loss that the city ever sustained. Then in the 15th century come the delightfully-named Jacobello del Fiore, the Vivarinis from Murano and – more significant than any of them – the patriarch Jacopo Bellini, his sons Gentile and Giovanni and his son-in-law Andrea Mantegna. Gentile Bellini and his younger contemporary Vittore (or Vettor in the Venetian dialect) Carpaccio have, beyond the slightest doubt, introduced more people to the sheer joy of Venetian art than any other two masters, above all for their several series of paintings representing the legendary histories of saints or relics which were regularly commissioned by the Scuole, or charitable religious brotherhoods, that played so important a part in the artistic life of the city. To Gentile we owe, *inter alia*, the greatest picture of the Piazza of San Marco ever painted – the vast canvas which forms one of the series on the Miracles of the Relic of the True Cross, commissioned by the Scuola di S. Giovanni Evangelista and now in the Accademia. Here too you may see in the same series Carpaccio's memorable portrayal of the old Rialto Bridge and, in the room opposite, his still more glorious St Ursula cycle, including the massacre of the saint's 11,000 virgins. Even then, however, it is not until you have visited the little Scuola di S. Giorgio degli Schiavoni that you will experience the full genius of this gayest, most graceful and most fanciful of painters.

With Giovanni Bellini we are back in the mainstream. Born around 1430 and living on until 1516, he leads the way into the High Renaissance and the golden age. With his fluency, his flawless technique and his profound Christian faith, he sometimes strikes me as the Bach of Venetian painting. If this analogy can be accepted, we might go on to describe Giorgione, the visionary young romantic who died at thirty-two, as its Schubert; Titian, with his immense range, his feeling for drama and his almost uncanny sureness of touch, as its Mozart; and Veronese, with his intensely Venetian love of colour, sumptuousness and opulence, as its Liszt. As for Tintoretto – austere, withdrawn, living only for his art, but a veritable powerhouse of energy and dynamism – he, there can be no doubt, is its Beethoven.

On the 17th century, silence is best. The spotlight shifts elsewhere, to Spain and the Low Countries; in Venice almost the only name worthy of mention is that of Sebastiano Ricci, who was not born until 1660 and spent most of his life abroad. But in the 18th, all the old genius flares up again. Canaletto, Bellotto and the Guardis demonstrated once again those qualities that Venice had marked for her own, celebrating their native city as no city had ever been celebrated before and handling perspective with a virtuosity which is revealed only to those foolhardy enough to try to recapture their effects by modern photography; while Giambattista Tiepolo regularly turned out canvases of such luminosity and radiance as to give one to suspect the existence of some hidden source of energy behind them.

In sculpture, we have only to think of the families of the delle Masagne – creators of the grand central window of the Doge's Palace, looking out over the Lagoon – the Lombardi and the Bon, of Jacopo Sansovino – by birth a Florentine, but a Venetian by adoption who spent his last forty-three years in Venice – and Alessandro Vittoria. As for architecture, here the achievement of the Venetians is perhaps the most awe-inspiring of all, by reason of their extraordinary ability to transform every succeeding architectural style into something entirely and unmistakably their own. Their first great building, the 11th-century Basilica of San Marco, is Byzantine through and through, modelled on Constantine the Great's Church of the Holy Apostles in Constantinople; but nothing remotely resembling its finished form was ever seen in Byzantium. Ruskin's description remains the best:

. . . beyond those troops of ordered arches there rises a vision out of the earth, and all the great square seems to have opened from it in a kind of awe, that we may see it far away; a multitude of pillars and white domes, clustered into a long low pyramid of coloured light; a treasureheap, it seems, partly of gold, and partly of opal and mother-of-pearl, hollowed beneath into five great vaulted porches, ceiled with fair mosaic, and beset with sculpture of alabaster, clear as amber and delicate as ivory – sculpture fantastic and involved, of palm leaves and lilies, and grapes and pomegranates, and birds clinging and fluttering among the branches, all twined together into an endless network of buds and plumes; and, in the midst of it, the solemn forms of angels, sceptred, and robed to the feet, and leaning to each other across the gates, their figures indistinct among the gleaming of the golden ground through the leaves beside them, interrupted and dim, like the morning light as it faded back among the branches of Eden, when first its gates were angel-guarded long ago. And round the walls of the porches there are set pillars of variegated stones, jasper and porphyry, and deep-green serpentine spotted with flakes of snow, and marbles, that half refuse and half yield to the sunshine, Cleopatra-like, 'their bluest veins to kiss' – the shadow, as it steals back from them, revealing line after line of azure undulation, as a receding tide leaves the waved sand; their capitals rich with interwoven tracery, rooted knots of herbage, and drifting leaves of acanthus and vine, and mystical signs, all beginning and ending in the Cross; and above them, in the broad archivolts, a continuous chain of language and life – angels, and the signs of heaven, and the labours of men, each in its appointed season upon the earth; and above these, another range of glittering pinnacles, mixed with white arches edged with scarlet flowers, a confusion of delight, amidst which the breasts of the Greek horses are seen blazing in their breadth of golden strength, and the St Mark's lion, lifted on a blue field covered with stars, until at last, as if in ecstasy, the crests of the arches break into a marble foam, and toss themselves far into the blue sky in flashes and wreaths of sculptured spray, as if the breakers on the Lido shore had been frost-bound before they fell, and the sea-nymphs had inlaid them with coral and amethyst.

With the coming of Gothic, a still more extraordinary metamorphosis took place; for the Venetians, by applying a style which we nowadays see as essentially ecclesiastical to secular building, once again evolved something uniquely their own – producing, in the Doge's Palace, one of the greatest architectural *tours de force* the world has to offer. The colour, to begin with, is magical, varying as it does from the palest apricot in the morning sun to the colour – and the apparent texture – of smoked salmon after a rainstorm. Beyond that, its beauty defies analysis: with all the weight on the upper storey and all the lightness below, it should look top-heavy; instead, the arcading always reminds me of a Victorian fringed tablecloth that just – but only just – touches the ground. But there remains one quality about this breathtaking building which always seems to me insufficiently stressed: its triumphant proclamation of the security of the nation. Remember first that this was not just the residence of the head of state; it was the nerve centre, not only of the city of Venice but of the entire Republic and

The peculiar acoustic properties of San Marco account in large part for the character of Venetian music. It could give a wonderfully rich and resonant sound, but only if the notes were prolonged and harmonically combined; double and treble choirs produced a specially thrilling effect. Complex counterpoint, however, was swamped, and this is as true today as it was in the time of the Gabrielis.

commercial Empire: it was, to make another analogy, Buckingham Palace, No. 10 Downing Street and the Palace of Westminster all combined. Now compare it with its equivalent in any other major Italian city: virtually everywhere else, the *palazzo pubblico* is a fortress, built for defence. Considering the constant warfare in mainland Italy throughout the middle ages, it could hardly have been anything else. Now look once again at the Doge's Palace. It could not keep out a Pekinese. Only Venice could afford such a building. Surrounded by her lagoon, looking resolutely eastward to Byzantium and the Orient, source of all her wealth, she could turn her back on the eternal bickering and internecine strife of the *terra firma*. She was safe, and she knew it.

The Renaissance came late to Venice. You will find the first glimmer of it if you go to the church of S. Zaccaria and – having gazed your fill at Giovanni Bellini's sublime altarpiece – make your way through to the little chapel of S. Tarasio on the south side. There in the vault you will see the frescoes of God the Father and his Saints, probably by Andrea del Castagno, certainly Florentine, and dated 1442. To find the equivalent in architecture, we have to wait another eighteen years – for Antonio Gambello to design the great archway to the Arsenal in 1460. By this time the Renaissance in Florence had been in progress for a century and a half; why were the Venetians so slow in following? Probably, I suspect, because they had acquired such mastery over their own particular brand of Gothic, and it suited them so well, that for a long time they saw no reason to change. But change they did, in the end – only to perform their usual conjuring trick by at once evolving a style which, although unquestionably Renaissance-inspired, somehow managed to be quintessentially Venetian at the same time. Once again they sought the elements they most loved – luxury and colour – going back to the old Byzantine habit of incrustation and adorning the exteriors with designs of glorious polychrome marble. Among churches, S. Maria dei Miracoli is probably the best example; among public buildings, the Scuola di San Marco; among palaces, the Ca' Dario on the Grand Canal.

With the coming of the 16th century this style – which we associate above all with the Lombardi family and Mauro Codussi – gives way to a rather purer form, exemplified by the work of Sansovino (notably the superb Marciana Library) and culminating with the arrival in the 1560s of Andrea Palladio. Of Palladio's Venetian churches, only one – the Redentore – remains exactly as he designed it; the façade of S. Giorgio Maggiore was actually completed, with several alterations, only thirty years after his death.

*　　*　　*

And so, finally, we come to music – the real subject of this book. And here again Venice's record is enough to leave us gasping. Not quite all the heroes of the pages that follow were natives of the city; but in almost every case Venice gave them shelter, or inspiration, or encouragement, or patronage, or a combination of the four; every one of them, I suspect, would have been proud to call himself at least an honorary Venetian, and a good many of them did.

Of all the arts, music knows the fewest frontiers; yet here too, as in every other field, Venice showed all her old, stubborn individuality. There was no logical

Francesco Gaffurio (1451–1522) was Milanese, but his De Harmonia Musicorum, *an influential text on musical theory, was republished in Venice in 1512.*

reason why San Marco should follow a different liturgy, requiring different music, from that of any other great church or cathedral in Christendom; but it did, and – as happened again and again in Venetian history – the Pope was obliged to accept the inevitable and give it his blessing. There was still less reason why Venetian music in the 18th century should have been the special preserve of female orphanages; and the results, it must be admitted, did not invariably impress foreign visitors. William Beckford, after a visit to the Mendicanti on August 27, 1780, could not resist noting:

The sight of the orchestra still makes me smile. You know, I suppose, it is entirely of the female gender; and that nothing is more common than to see a delicate white hand journeying across an enormous double bass, or a pair of roseate cheeks puffing with all their efforts at a french-horn. Some of them who are grown old and Amazonian, have abandoned their fiddles and their lovers, and take vigorously to the kettle-drum; and one poor limping lady, who had been crossed in love, now makes an admirable figure on the bassoon.

At their best, however, at the Pietà under Vivaldi or the Incurabili under Galuppi, these girls could enchant all those who heard them – and they were certainly admired and respected in Venice: where else, after all, could one hope to find a bronze plaque like that affixed to the outside of the south wall of the Pietà, calling down the threat of *fulmination* – being struck by lightning – on anyone who attempts to pass off his legitimate daughter as an illegitimate one in order to get her accepted into the music school?

For in Venice – far more, surely, than in any other city in Italy – music mattered; indeed, it still matters today, just as it has for the past five hundred years. Would it have been possible, I wonder, to make five fifty-minute television films for the general public on as many centuries of music in Rome, or Milan, or Florence, or even Naples? It seems unlikely. In all other cities of the West, the 20th century intrudes to an almost impossible degree. Only Venice has been preserved; for that same *cordon sanitaire* of shallow water that the first Venetians chose for their protection has served, in our own day, to defend them from the greatest scourge of modern urban life, the motor car. Had it not done so, for many years already the Piazza San Marco would have been transformed into one enormous car park. Nor is it just the Piazza that has survived: the ultimate miracle is that the whole of Venice has come down to us almost unscathed, a priceless historical document, without equal in the world.

That is why working on this project has been, for all of us who have been associated with it, such a memorable experience. Though music has been our primary concern, we have tried always to keep it within its context: to relate it to the composers who wrote it, to the musicians who played and sang it, and above all to the city that gave it birth. In doing so we have been guided by an equally memorable man. He is, first and foremost, one of the great scholars of his day, one whose knowledge and understanding of the whole history of western music is probably unparalleled; but he is also an enthusiast, whose enthusiasm is effortlessly transmitted to all those who come within his formidable range. He educated us, he inspired us, he made us laugh. And he wrote this book.

JOHN JULIUS NORWICH

I The Sixteenth Century

By the year 1500 Venice could already look back on a long and glorious history. Her origins had been humble indeed, when the shoals and sandbanks of her lagoon had provided nothing more than a refuge from the barbarian invasions; but by the middle of the 8th century she had won effective independence from Byzantium and was rapidly evolving, under her elected Doge, that unique political system which was to endure for nearly a thousand years. Economically too she was beginning to prosper, as her merchantmen became increasingly numerous throughout the Eastern Mediterranean. What she lacked above all in those early years was status: her older neighbours still looked upon her as a nouveau-riche, a jumped-up parvenu unworthy of serious consideration. All this was changed, however, when in 828 two Venetian merchants stole the body of St Mark from its shrine in Alexandria and brought it back in triumph to the Rialto. It was not consigned, as might have been expected, to the cathedral: this would have put it too much in the power of the Church. Instead, a great basilica was built especially to contain it, adjoining the Palace of the Doge and serving technically as his private chapel – a status it was to preserve for as long as the Republic lasted. Thenceforth Venice was to be a place of pilgrimage as well as of trade, while her ruler was accepted by the princes of Europe as one of themselves.

Trade, however, continued to predominate – as Venice showed again and again during the period of the Crusades, in the first three of which she remained on the sidelines except when her own commercial interests were involved. In the Fourth, on the other hand, she played the leading part, and was chiefly responsible for turning the Crusading army (for which she had provided the ships) away from Saracen-held Palestine and against Christian Constantinople. In consequence the magnificent city was sacked and looted, its Greek Emperors being replaced by a line of Frankish thugs who in fifty years reduced the once-great Empire to a state of ruin from which it never properly recovered; Venice, however, gained for herself not only the centre of Constantinople but all the western coast of Greece, together with the Ionian Islands, the Peloponnese, much of the Aegean and the all-important island of Crete. Her Doge, meanwhile, added to his many honorifics an additional title: Lord of a Quarter and Half a Quarter of the Roman Empire.

By the 15th century the Republic had reached the summit of its power. All too soon, however, the decline began. Already the Ottoman Turks had established themselves in Eastern Europe and had mopped up most of the Balkan peninsula. Steadily they pushed their frontiers forward, until on Tuesday, 29 May 1453 the young Sultan Mehmet II smashed down the walls of Constantinople and put an end, after 1123 years, to the Byzantine Empire. Steadily, too, they absorbed Venice's trading colonies in the Mediterranean, cutting her lines of communication and supply, relentlessly sapping her power. Then, as the century drew to its

4   The most powerful influence upon Venetian 16th-century music was probably Orlando Lassus. Lassus (or di Lasso, or De Lattre; he was Flemish) had himself spent several years in Italy before settling in Munich, where he directed Albrecht V's court orchestra. Here, from 1560 to 1564 Andrea Gabrieli stayed, learning all he could and going back to Venice a master of the northern style. A contemporary painting of the Munich court orchestra shows Lassus standing on the extreme left and an ensemble of musicians with their instruments — keyboard, strings, woodwind and brass — depicted in realistic detail. Lassus himself was in Venice in 1574.

close, there came a still greater blow: in 1499 Vasco da Gama landed at Lisbon, having made the return journey to the Indies via the Cape of Good Hope. Overnight, Venice had become a backwater.

Meanwhile, as the East had become more and more inaccessible, the West had beckoned. Venice now found herself, almost to her surprise, a mainland power — mistress of a considerable area of north-east Italy. It was not however an unmixed blessing, involving her as it did in that seemingly endless warfare which characterizes north Italian history at this time, and frequently incurring the hostility of lands far beyond the Alps. In 1508, indeed, with the formation of the League of Cambrai, she found the Pope, the Holy Roman Emperor and what was virtually the whole of Western Christendom united against her.

Venice, it seemed, had lost her way. Her sureness of touch was gone. On terra firma, she spent vast fortunes on mercenary armies and condottiere generals to fight her battles for her across the plain of Lombardy and beyond; at sea, she continued her long and desperate struggle against the Turk but was never able to stem his advance for long. In 1570 Cyprus fell; her general, Marcantonio Bragadin, after making honorable terms for his surrender, was betrayed by the Turkish commander and flayed alive. In the following year, Venice and her Papal and Spanish allies took their revenge, utterly destroying the Turkish fleet at Lepanto, the last great naval engagement in history to be fought with oared galleys. But her victory made little difference. She failed to regain Cyprus and only two years later concluded a separate peace with the Sultan, relinquishing all claims to the island.

And yet, strangely enough, it was precisely at this time of commercial decline, political uncertainty and military reversals that her artistic and cultural life began to flourish as never before. The 15th century had witnessed the first superb flowering of her painting and her architecture; the 16th was to see those arts — and others — developing into their full maturity. By 1500, too, she had become the intellectual centre of Italy, a city in which more books had been produced than in Rome, Milan, Florence and Naples combined; it was in Venice, in 1490, that Aldus Manutius had set up his presses in the Campo S. Agostino and had begun the task that was to occupy him for the next twenty-five years: that of editing, printing and publishing the whole canon of Greek classical literature. Where the Aldine Press led, many others followed; and though the city was never to make a major contribution to world literature, no other did more to spread it abroad. Meanwhile — as we have already seen in the Introduction — Venetian painters were dazzling all Europe, Venetian sculptors were producing superb statuary, while Venetian architects were erecting some of the most exquisite and sumptuous churches and palaces that even Venice could boast. By 1600 Venice was, as far as her astonished visitors could judge, more opulent than ever.

And then there was the music . . .

ECCLES
XXXII
SICVT IN FABRICA
ONE AVRI SIGNVM
EST SMARAGDI SIC
NVMERVS MVSICORV
IN IVCVNO ET
MODERATO
VINO

5   *Adrian Willaert was, like Lassus, a Fleming, but after travelling widely in central Europe and Italy he was appointed* maestro di cappella *at San Marco in 1527, when this portrait (RIGHT) was painted. He died there in 1562, aged over 80. Famous as a composer and teacher, he seems to have initiated the practice of using a double choir to exploit the special qualities of San Marco, setting a style that Andrea and Giovanni Gabrieli were to follow.*

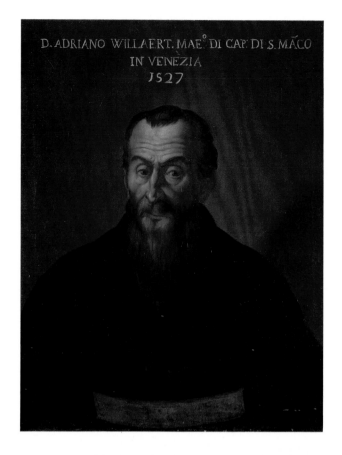

6   *Giovanni Pierluigi Palestrina, 1525–94, is generally considered the greatest composer of the 16th century. His influential adoption of the new, simpler word-setting demanded by the church counteracted the intricacies of the Flemish style.*

7   OPPOSITE *Giovanni Gabrieli, like his uncle Andrea, spent several years in Germany with Lassus, from 1575 to 1584. The year after he returned he took over as* maestro di cappella. *His talents blossomed. He wrote music for all occasions, sacred and secular, greatly extending the use of instrumental music to accompany the voice. He was also a skilled organist and lute player, and is portrayed here, no doubt by his own choice, as a gentleman lutanist.*

8   *Gentile Bellini painted his famous picture of* The Procession of the Cross *in the Piazza San Marco in 1496. The reliquary which contains the fragment of the Cross is in the centre under the canopy. The band of* pifferi *is on the extreme right.*

9   In defining the nature of the various schools of Italian art, critics have characterized the Florentines as predominantly intellectual and the Venetians as concerned with the world of the senses. Their pictures dwell lovingly on the pleasures of sight, touch, taste . . . and hearing. Music permeates Venetian art, from the purely mundane to the supernaturally angelic.
LEFT *Titian's* Concert *is almost a celebration of the intimacy produced by private music-making.*

10, 11, 12   *Titian's young girl in his allegory of* The Ages of Man (ABOVE) *holds two recorders tuned to different pitches.* LEFT The Concert *by Ambrosius Benson shows an early type of violin with straight sides.* OPPOSITE *Bonifacio de 'Pitati's* Dives and Lazarus *chooses to represent Dives' riches almost entirely in terms of music. In the far background on the right a dog drives away the beggar Lazarus.*

I PRELUDE 1500–1550

Towards the end of the 15th century, a vast programme of building began in Venice. Visitors passing through the Republic commented on the rapid rate of change as churches, palazzi and public buildings sprang up all over the city. Palladio created beautiful churches, the Lombardi embellished them with breathtaking sculptures, whilst Bellini, Titian, Tintoretto and Veronese painted pictures rich in colour and design. Venice's greatest age of art and architecture was in full flow.

None could fail to be impressed. And it was vital for Venice that they should be. To maintain her position in the changing world about her, she could no longer rely on her commercial wealth, nor on her navy, nor on the proud, swaggering condottieri of the previous century. If she were to survive, she must have peace; and peace, in its turn depended on neutrality in the struggles which continued, as they always had, to tear Europe apart. But neutrality itself was hard to preserve against the pressures to which she was increasingly subjected – from Emperor and Pope, Frenchman and Spaniard, Austrian and Turk. It could be maintained only by the most subtle diplomacy; and diplomats must always speak, or appear to speak, from a position of strength.

Thus, more than ever before, Venice needed the respect of her more powerful neighbours; and none knew better than she the importance, in this regard, of the face which she presented to the world. This is not to say that she would not always have decked herself out as gorgeously as she was able, or that she would ever have resented money spent on her own self-glorification; far from it. The splendour of Venice can never be dismissed as a confidence trick. But like any great beauty, she was acutely conscious of the effect that beauty had on others; and she used it to the full.[1]

In the pursuit of this beauty, the Republic's long-standing reputation for tolerance was invaluable. Fiercely protective of her individuality, the Republic had withstood all attempts by Rome to subject her to its iron rule, and was in consequence widely respected as a centre of great personal freedom. Pietro Aretino wrote:

13, 14 *The Scuola di San Marco. Its façade of 1533–43 is an example of the pre-Palladio style in Venice, with its emphasis on marble decoration and* trompe-l'oeil *perspectives. It is now the Ospedale Civile. These two views, by Bellotto in the mid 18th century and today, demonstrate how miraculously little Venice has changed.*

Here treason has no place. Here favour in high circles does no wrong to be set right. Here no cruel mistress reigns. Here the insolent and effeminate give no commands. Here no one robs, coerces or murders. O hostelry of all the dispersed and exiled, how much greater would be the woes of Italy if your bounty were any the less! Here stands a refuge for all her nations. Here her wealth may be kept in safety. Venice opens her arms to all whom others shun. She lifts up all whom others abase. She welcomes those whom others persecute. She cheers the mourner in his grief and defends the despised and the destitute with charity and love. And so I bow to Venice with good reason. She is a living reproach to Rome.[2]

The two sides of Venetian life — the dark and the light. Behind the gaiety lay a ruthlessly-enforced obedience to authority, against which the ordinary citizen had little redress. The beautiful little Bridge of Sighs (RIGHT) connected the Ducal Palace, where justice was administered, to the state prison on the other side of the canal. It was built in the 16th century by Antonio Contino.

Venice is a city of bridges. Another forms the centrepiece of Gentile Bellini's painting (FAR RIGHT) of an incident when a piece of the True Cross accidentally fell into the canal and was miraculously rescued. The procession on it includes musicians (in the middle to the right of the banner) who have stopped playing in consternation. In the water Andrea Vendramin, Grand Guardian of the guild which owned it, triumphantly holds the recovered reliquary. On the right are the soberly-dressed patrician patrons.

The letter-box into which Venetian citizens could slip anonymous denunciations.

Greatest of Venetian printers
was Aldus Manutius, whose
device was the dolphin and
anchor, signifying 'Festina
Lente' (speed combined with
caution). Aldus came to Venice
in 1490 and died there in 1515.
During that time he printed the
first editions of twenty-eight
Greek and Latin classics.
Scholars from all over Europe
were drawn to Venice because of
his reputation. Erasmus wrote:
'Venice, so famous on so many
accounts, is most famous because
of the Aldine press.'

This letter, written by Aretino, who was a Roman citizen, to the Doge, undoubtedly exaggerates. Venice, like most of its neighbours, was a police state which sought to control most aspects of its citizens' lives. The Serenissima *expected* every man, woman and child in the territory to give his or her whole self to the public weal. It regulated the clothes they wore (though with limited success): procurators were allowed to wear red damask togas with stoles over their left shoulders; prefects wore a similar robe but without the stole; members of the great council were limited in the amount of jewelry they wore, and it was severely prohibited for the people to wear gold. Travel abroad was restricted. The populace was forbidden to have any contact with foreigners. The Serenissima encouraged denunciations, and there was a special kind of letter-box in the ducal palace for that purpose. Crimes against the state were hideously punished; the Bridge of Sighs leading to the grim prison was infamous. People were tortured in a special room set up near the Council and often in the early morning, on the piazzetta, the broken remains of a criminal who had died shrieking in agony were exposed as a warning to the populace. As Hugh Honour observes, 'Such regimentation supported, and was supported by, the Venetian passion for anonymity, or submission to the personality of the State . . . [most artists] are very nearly as anonymous as the artists who created the mosaics in San Marco or the stone masons who raised its fabric'.[3]

Nevertheless, in relation to its neighbours, and to Rome in particular, Venice was a paradise of personal freedom. Many printers were attracted to Venice by its low level of censorship – during the early 16th century there were no less than sixty-five presses in the city, three times as many as in Rome and six times as many as in Florence. Thus Venice, whilst producing no great literature herself, was the centre of Italian intellectual activity in the first half of the 16th century, exporting books far and wide.

Just as literature benefited from Venice's independent stand against Rome, so did music. Although the Republic was nominally Roman Catholic it had retained many local idiosyncrasies within its liturgy and also placed a far greater emphasis on the link between God and the State than was common elsewhere. Many of the Roman Catholic feast days had come to be associated with great events in the Republic's history and were therefore given far greater emphasis than normal; St Mark's day was celebrated in style because St Mark was the Republic's protector: St Isidore's feast day marked an occasion when La Serenissima had been delivered from great danger; St Vitus' and Modestus' day commemorated the discovery of a plot against the Republic, etc. In total some forty special feast days were celebrated each year.

Each involved elaborate ceremonies in which the laity took the principal place. Sir Richard Torkington describes the most famous of these ceremonies, the Ascension Day feast (in which the Doge celebrates the Republic's close association with the sea by throwing a ring into the waters) in 1517.

The Duke with grett Triumphe and solemnyte with all the Senyorye went in ther Archa trimuphali, which ys in maner of a sayle of a straange facion and wonder stately . . .

And so they rowed in to the see, with the assistens of ther Patriarche, And ther Spoused the see with a ryng. The spousall words be In signum veri perpetuique Domini.

The Apotheosis of Venice, by Paolo Veronese. Venetian art was largely devoted to what we should call state propaganda. Here Venice, personified as a beautiful and richly-dressed woman, is crowned by Victory as she sits in the clouds amidst the gods and goddesses of Olympus. Underneath, in the earthly realm, lords, ladies, officials and soldiers celebrate her triumph.

And therwith the Duke lete fall the ryng in to the see, the processe and the ceremonyes whereof war to long to wryte.

Thanne thaye Rode to the Abbey of Seynt Nicholas to blake Monkys that stond by juste be them, And all thaye brake ther fastes, And so retornyd a geyne to Venys, To the Dukys palace, Where they had provyd for them a mervelows Dyner, wher at we Pilgrymes war present and see them servyd. At which Dyner her was viii Corse of soundery metys, And att every Corse the Trunpettes and the mynystrellys com inne a for them.[4]

Over a century later R. Lassels wrote of ceremonies in Venice:

In the festive occasions the hero is not the saint whose day is being celebrated, still less any individual Venetian: it is Venice itself. The role of the Doge as guardian rather than ruler was emphasised at his election; he was taken to the place where the body of his predecessor had recently been lying in the church of SS Giovanni e Paolo, and told that his body would lie there before long. The feasts of Venice thus reiterated many times a year a lesson which can scarcely have been lost on the populace at large; and care was taken to involve them in such a way that they too felt some stake in their most serene Republic.[5]

*Disastrous fires in 1574 and 1577 (ABOVE)
destroyed much of the interior of the Ducal Palace,
but made possible its rebuilding in the Renaissance
style, then only just taking root in Venice. One of
the parts left intact was the Golden Staircase
(RIGHT) leading from the gallery of the courtyard
to the Doge's apartments. It is decorated with gilt
stucco (hence the name) and fresco. The Sala del
Collegio (OPPOSITE) was entirely rebuilt after
the fire of 1574 to designs by Palladio and others.
Here ambassadors and distinguished foreigners were
received.*

ABOVE RIGHT: *the nave of S. Giorgio Maggiore,
begun in 1566 by Andrea Palladio and finished
after his death. Palladio's works mark a breach
with Venetian tradition, clearly expressing the
classical Renaissance that had begun in Florence a
century earlier and pointing forward to the future.*

CANONICI · SCVDIERI DEL DOGE · CAMERARII SERENISIMI PRINCIPE

Sansovino in *Venetia Citta Novilissima*, 1663, writes: 'It has always been our custom to accompany the religious with the temporal.'[6]

The Doge, the symbolical head of state, and the Signory attended mass at San Marco. There were five classes of service:

1　No musicians
2　Half the choir singing *a capella* (lower tiers only)
3　Half the choir singing with organ accompaniment
4　The full choir, 2 organs and half the orchestra, performing in the upper lofts as well as the lower tiers.
5　The full choir, all the organs and the full orchestra, performing.

Once the mass was over the procession would begin, in the following order:

1　At the front, eight standards which had been presented to the Republic by the Pope.
2　Heralds blowing silver trumpets, held up in front on the shoulders of several youths. These heralds, or *Praecones*, went in pairs, clothed in turquoise blue and long cloaks, with red *berretta* on their heads bearing a small gold medallion impressed with the figure of St Mark.
3　Pairs of players with trombones, clad in red, playing harmoniously all the way.
4　The Squires of the Doge, dressed in black velvet.
5　Six canons wearing priest's vestments.
6　The Stewards of the Doge.

TROMBE PIFEARI | TVBÆ ET BARB.I TON | SERVITORI DELL'IMBASCIATORI | ORATOR FAM.

7   Secretaries of the College.
8   The Senate.
9   The Council of Ten.
10 Those Chancellors of the Doge called *inferiors* and *ducali* according to the degree of their service to the Republic.
11 The Grand Chancellor.
12 The Chaplain of the Doge with the bearer of the Ducal Cap who carries a candle, with the Doge's Page.
13 The ceremonial Chair and Cushion on each side of the Doge's umbrella.
14 The Doge in person, wearing an ermine cape, with the ambassadors of foreign princes.
15 The Councillors and Procurators of San Marco, the judges, the army council, and the other senators and civil authorities, all clad in crimson silk.

Thus priests, Doge, Signory and the incipient bourgeoisie of the confraternities were all brought together to worship God, and the everlasting City Republic.

In all this, music played a very important part. Such pomp and splendour needed to be accompanied by sound, and sound which would be as colourful, rich and idiosyncratic as the procession itself. Numbers of singers and instrumentalists were employed for the festivals (as Bellini's famous picture of a Corpus Domini procession of 1490 shows). Motet texts from other Italian cities tell us of musical celebrations for the accession of princes, weddings, peace treaties and many other important events. In Venice there was the opportunity to practise this art continuously. The frequency of these events (some 40 a year!) meant that composers had to become experts in the genre.

This report by Sir Henry Wotton, the English Ambassador in Venice, in 1622, illustrates just how important the role of music was on these feast days, since the absence of music from one year's celebration of San Rocco's day could be used as propaganda by the Vatican.

Among other notes of this week, let me tell your Lordship that we have seen one great solecism, a St. Rocco's Day uncelebrated with music, even their peculiar Saint; which in common discourse is attributed either to the avarice or the spite of an apothecary, on whom that confraternity did lay the charge of those rites this year against his will. This omission to many ears may perchance sound like a trifle; but the Pope's instruments work upon it, and say it is no marvel if his authority be decayed here (as hath been lately seen in violating the Court of Inquisition, and in a round proceeding against the Bishop of Padova) when their own saints (for Rocco is not yet in the Roman Canon) are so slighted.[7]

The musical staff of San Marco varied in size from century to century but the basis was as follows:

1   *Maestro di cappella*: his task was to oversee and direct all musical performances. At most times he was a well known composer with a comfortable salary and free lodging near the Piazza.
2   Vice *maestro di cappella*: This post existed from 1607 onwards. It was the vice-maestro's task to conduct the first choir in polychoral works.
3   *Maestro di concerti*: he conducted the second choir.
4   Organists: There were two organists from the end of the 15th century onwards. They alternated week by week. Only on special feast days would both organists be required. In the 17th century it had become the practice for the lessons at Matins on Wednesday, Thursday and Friday of Holy Week to be accompanied by harpsichord. It was the task of the second organist to play the harpsichord. In 1588 a chamber organ was added and from the middle of the 17th century there were two chamber organists.
5   Caretaker for the organs.
6   The choir: in the 16th century this had 16 members, in the 17th century 36; in the 18th century 24. Each singer was paid up to 100 ducats a year.
7   A music copyist.
8   Custodian of the choir books.
9   Beat tapper.
10   Pitch giver.

All the members of the musical staff were paid at intervals of two months by the *maestro di cappella*.

Their contracts were for three or four years, reviewed each July. In the era of Monteverdi the fines for absence were 2 ducats (on major feast days) and 1 ducat for absence from a procession. On all other occasions absence led to a fine of one twentieth of the musician's annual salary. There was an *appuntadore* who recorded attendance and collected fines.

Otto Stendardi. Comandadori. Sci trombe de argento. Serui de l'Ambasciatori.
Piffari.

Scudieri del dogc.

Caualier.

Secretarij

Stocho. Ombrela. Ambasciator Cesareo. Cusino.
Dogc.

Balotin. Diacono.

Capelà

Catedra.

altri Ambasciatori Legato. Cancelier grande. Capitano grande.

Illustrisima Signoria.

PROCESSIONE GENERALE FATTA IN VI:
nella publicatione della Lega l'anno M. D. LXXI.

Il Ser.mo Prencipe con la Signoria il giorno di Natale ascolta Vespro in S. Georgio Magiore et il di seguente ua alla Messa
in detta Chiesa in contrato et accompagnato al rittorno dall'Abbate et Cap.to de quelli RR. Monaci Questo celebre tempio
fu ordinato dal Palladio Architetto Eccel.mo etc posto in isola a dirimpeto della Piazza d.S. Marco, et e tenuto uno de famosi tempij d'Italia
franco forma con priuilegio

The two most important positions were those of *maestro di cappella* and first organist. To be an organist at San Marco was an honour to which few of that profession could aspire. Their position was not normally of great distinction – in most churches the organist was rarely both player of his instrument and *magister chori* as we would expect today. This latter role (better paid and more respected) usually belonged to a promoted singer who had also mastered the art of composition. Titlepages of books of masses and motets reveal relatively few organists among their composers. The two skills (*magister chori* and keyboard player) were separate. The fame of the organists was transient and little music was published for them in the 16th century; a choir needs several copies of a motet, an organist only one of a canzona.

Two Venetian churches famous for their music.
OPPOSITE *S. Giorgio Maggiore*, seen here in a woodcut of a Doge arriving for Vespers at Easter; note the woodwind players and trombonists in the boats.
ABOVE *S. Maria Gloriosa dei Frari*, the main church of the Franciscan mendicant order. Monteverdi is buried here.

But in Venice, and especially in San Marco, organists were valued. There had been an organist in the basilica for more than a century before the *maestro di cappella*'s post had been established. Tradition decreed the continuance of this post, at a decent salary, even when the vogue for the Netherlands composers had suggested surrender to the ways of other courts. Venice had some extraordinarily good organists – Annibale Padovano, Andrea Gabrieli, Claudio Merulo. Merulo left Venice for Parma, near his native Correggio, but not before he had taught his skill to a considerable number of Venetian pupils, who formed an essentially Venetian school of organ playing.

San Marco was not the only centre of musical activity in Venice. Churches abounded in Venice, and many of them employed an organist. A few also employed a *maestro di cappella*, and it was common practice for churches to hire singers and players for special feast days. Two of San Marco's closest rivals on the music scene were Santa Maria Gloriosa dei Frari, and SS. Giovanni e Paolo.

Santa Maria Gloriosa dei Frari had a regular position for a *maestro di cappella* throughout the 16th and 17th centuries. The Frari also had one principal organ and a chamber organ. Its instrumental ensembles consisted of trombones, spinets, bass viols, violins, lutes and shawms, though the patriarchal edict of 1633, concerning the text and instruments that could be used in sacred works, reduced this to lute, theorbo and harp. By the end of the 17th century, the Frari's main concern was musical theory.

The Dominican church of SS. Giovanni e Paolo employed an organist (Cavalli was organist there from 1620–1630), and was the scene of several grand spectacles involving music by Monteverdi and Cavalli. The churches of Santo Stefano, San Salvador and Madonna dell'Orto in Cannaregio all employed musicians for special occasions.

Another source of great musical activity was the *scuole grande* of the Venetian Confraternities. The Institution of the *scuola grande*, as developed by the 16th century, was unique to Venice. The confraternities had originated in the 13th century as lay brotherhoods dedicated to flagellating themselves in procession, to atone for the sins of mankind and to prepare themselves for death. By the 16th century the Venetian brothers were mostly merchants who favoured less primitive ways of reminding themselves of redemption and of seeking grace. The confraternities became vehicles for the relief of the poor and sick, and for the patronage of the arts to the greater glory of God.

The confraternities (scuole) were institutions founded for various charitable purposes. In Venice they became extremely rich and powerful and it was under their patronage that music was able to make some of its most valuable advances. RIGHT *the Scuola di S. Giovanni Evangelista, one of the leading* scuole *in Venice.* OPPOSITE *the hall of the Scuola di S. Rocco, with paintings by Tintoretto.*

Thomas Coryat wrote in 1608:

The third feast was upon Saint Roches day being Saturday and the sixth day of August, where I heard the best musicke that ever I did in all my life both in the morning and the afternoone, so good that I would willingly goe an hundred miles a foote at any time to hear the like. The place where it was, is neare to Saint Roches Church, a very sumptuous and magnificent building that belongeth to one of the sixe Companies of the Citie. For there are in Venice sixe Fraternities of Companies that have their several halles (as we call them in London) belonging to them, a great maintenance for the performing of these shewes that each company dothe make . . . In this (the lowest) roome are two or three faire Altars. For this roome is not appointed for merriments and banquetings as the religion, therein to laud and prayse god and his Saints with Psalmes, Hymnes, spirituall song and melodious musicke upon daies dedicated unto Saintes.[8]

The confraternities could alleviate poverty, help the sick, see that orphans were provided for. In addition they acted as an 'insurance' for their paying members: sick pay, masses for the dead, and dowries for the daughters of the less affluent

were available as 'perks' for the members who had joined the club specifically to achieve greater security.

They also commissioned paintings, dramas and music and were required to provide a company of singers and instrumentalists for state processions. For this purpose they employed small bands of musicians. These players were not very well paid, and were not generally of top quality. The players most commonly mentioned as employees of the confraternities are called *sonadori di lironi*. *Lirone* could refer to the *lira da braccio*, an instrument especially suitable for al fresco processions, since it could play chords as well as single melodic lines. All the instruments had to be portable. The players performed only in the processions – it is unlikely that they would have taken part in the Mass.

In times of hardship the confraternities stressed their charitable functions. Orders went out to reduce expenditure on anything except the giving of alms. Singers or players would be laid off, either the whole company being dismissed or their numbers being reduced. Sometimes new taxes forced the governing body of the confraternity to take such steps. But on the whole the demands of the state worked to increase the expenditure on pomp and splendour.

Organists were the most highly-honoured musicians since they were the key figures in performances of the mass. This portrait of the organist and teacher Claudio Merulo, crowned with a laurel wreath, was painted in 1604.

In 1585 the Council of Ten ordered the Scuole to increase their expenditure on a special San Marco's Day procession to celebrate the peace treaty between France and Spain. During the interdict of 1606-7 the state encouraged them to show how well these Venetian institutions could do without Papal support.

Music in Europe was undergoing a major change. This was the age of the Reformation. Martin Luther had pinned his ninety-five theses to the door of the church at Wittenberg in 1517 and thus began a major movement against the Roman Catholic Church, a movement which was adopted, for political and religious reasons, by much of northern Europe.

The Emperor Charles V held out hopes, in the middle of the 16th century, that some miracle might heal the breach between Catholics and Protestants. A Protestant delegation went to the Council of Trent in 1551 but nothing could be done; the division was irrevocable. The division soon became allied with national interests. Catholicism maintained its position in southern Europe, whereas Lutheranism remained rooted in Teutonic lands, and Calvinism was thinly distributed in Scotland, France and the Netherlands and was stretching towards Poland and Hungary.

In this conflict music was heavily involved. Music played a considerable role in the expression of religious belief and the main employer of composers and musicians was the Church. The new Protestant religion, seeking to find new forms of musical expression to suit its creed, produced in Germany the sturdy Lutheran chorales, sung by the whole congregation. This was a blow at the Latin Catholic church services, in the music of which the faithful hardly participated. 'Ein feste Burg ist unser Gott' (A mighty fortress is our God) was heady stuff, and it put Catholic music in some quandary.

Catholics gathered at the Council of Trent to draw up a strategy to counteract Protestantism. Music was high on the agenda. The Protestants had criticised Catholic music: for its use of secular melodies, even love songs, as the basis for Holy Mass; for the wild exhibitionism of virtuoso organists; and for the intricate Flemish polyphony, so complex that the text became not only obscured but virtually incomprehensible. They argued that Catholic church music had strayed far from its original purpose – the praise and worship of God.

The Council of Trent's response to these criticisms was to adopt a new musical style, 'homophonic polyphony', in which the text was always easily intelligible and the music reflected the meaning of the words.

By the late 16th century the evolution of musical imagery to match the words was far advanced. The reformers insisted that in church music there should be as far as possible 'for every syllable a note'. Among the many offerings in this new style, the one that became intimately associated with it was the *Missa Papae Marcelli* by Giovanni Pierluigi da Palestrina (c. 1525–1594), *maestro di cappella* at Sta Maria Maggiore at Rome.

By 1590, the movement was virtually over, but its influence went beyond the aims of reformers. Church composers paid more attention to the enunciation of the words. Their musical rhythms and phrases stem from verbal accentuation and the normal rhythms and phrases of speech.

The major force in 16th century music north of the Alps was certainly Lassus, or Orlando di Lasso as he Italianized his name. He was born at Mons about 1532

Orlando Lassus, or di Lasso, the most distinguished musician of his age, was born in Flanders but spent much of his life in Germany and acquired a European reputation. He deeply influenced Andrea Gabrieli and through him the whole course of music in Venice. This edition of his First Book of Madrigals was published there in 1557.

and travelled widely, being appointed *maestro di cappella* at St John Lateran in Rome for a while. He was a trilingual, speaking German, French and Italian like a native, and this internationalism is reflected in his truly polyglot music. His chansons are delectable, witty, heartfelt; his madrigals are as fine as any, and his works for church are models of their kind and were circulated all over civilized Europe. He was a universal man, like Mozart.

Venice in the 16th century could boast neither a Palestrina nor a Lassus, but it nevertheless played a significant role in the development of music. Under the aegis of its three greatest composers of that period, Willaert and Andrea and Giovanni Gabrieli, it was the scene of two major developments: polychoral church music, leading to polyphonic instrumental music.

Polychoral music was a result largely of the physical nature of San Marco, and the necessity to use music both for masses and processions. San Marco was a vast building with two organs set in lofty galleries. The intricacies of the Flemish polyphonic style would have been swallowed up in the church's cavernous depths. Also, the size of the church, and the need to move the choirs in procession, created problems of coordination. The Venetian composers therefore adopted a much simpler, homophonic style, which emphasised the words and the sonority of the human voice. This led to a tendency to use more voices, with an increase in overall tessitura. The use of two choirs, placed in different parts of the church, began.

The basilica of San Marco was the centre of Venetian musical life right up to the beginning of the 19th century, and its maestro di cappella was the acknowledged leader of his profession. Foreign visitors were always impressed by the players and singers of San Marco, and also by the acoustic properties of the building itself, where the various domes and spaces gave splendid opportunities for antiphonal effects and divided groups. LEFT AND BELOW a piffaro and singer of San Marco. OPPOSITE the northern pulpit of San Marco, with a view behind it of one of the galleries and domes. These galleries were regularly used for double choirs singing together.

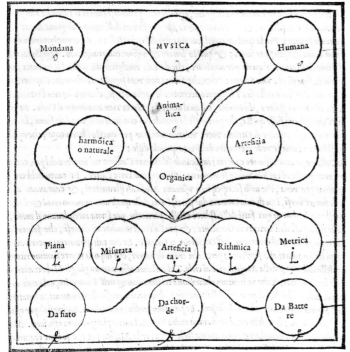

Gioseffo Zarlino, maestro di cappella *at San Marco in the late 16th century, was not only a teacher and performer but an early theoretician of music. His system relates different kinds of sounds and rhythms to sensory and spiritual perceptions, culminating in the art of 'Musica' itself.*

The roots of double-choir music are usually thought to lie in the psalm settings which Willaert published in 1550, *Di Adriano et di Jachet: I salmi appertinenti alli Vesperi . . . a duoi chori.* The basses of the two choirs were essentially the same, though sometimes an octave apart. This effectively reduced an eight-part texture to seven parts and is the first hint of a consciousness that doubling parts is needed at times to adjust the balance – the beginnings of the modern idea of orchestration.

The divided choir naturally led to a division of material. Instead of true counterpoint, two choirs treated as distant entities gave rise to distinct phrases. The choirs could be segregated, each initiating new ideas or repeating those already stated. Andrea Gabrieli's early motets merely divided the parts of the choirs equally, but in later motets he would divide the parts along different melodic lines, using trombones and cornets of the new permanent ensemble at San Marco, and violins and shawms (part-time) to balance the sound. His nephew, Giovanni, extended this use further, and began writing entirely instrumental pieces based on the motet style, but gradually developing melodic phrasing suited to instrumental as opposed to vocal expression. With this development came the establishment of an orchestra at San Marco.

The first permanent instrumental ensemble was founded in 1568. The Procurators hired Girolamo Dalla Casa (called da Udine, c. 1543–1601) to give concerts with his two brothers and other musicians in the organ lofts. This had been recommended by Zarlino, who had been appointed *maestro di cappella* three years earlier.

Girolamo da Udine was left to find other players to make up the ensemble; it seems unlikely that it consisted of more than three or four during the 1570s. Extra musicians were engaged when necessary.[9]

Their stipend was not very large compared with that of the singers, i.e. the social status of the flute players, or *piffari*, was not to be compared with that of employees of the church. They also were not expected to attend so frequently. The singers were supposed – though they often did not – to sing daily.

In comparison to other cities the formation of this permanent ensemble was late. The reason for this delay lies with the organization of Venetian institutions. For many years six silver trumpets accompanied the Doge on his processional visits throughout the city. (The Doge paid for these out of his own pocket.) These silver trumpets fulfilled one of the functions of the *piffari* in other towns where public show demanded them as symbols of authority rather than for any musical purpose. They also went into church and took part in the Mass or Vespers.

The main purpose of the new players was to swell the sound in the sung parts of mass and vespers. Whether they played independently of the choir, and if so what they played, remains uncertain. Descriptions from the era do not go into such details, telling us merely that instruments were used. There is a wealth of information about the practice of the 17th century, but how far can this be applied to a previous era? The surviving repertory of instrumental music is small. The Venetian publishing houses were printing music for the instrumental ensemble in some quantity from about 1550 onwards but it seems to be teaching material rather than music for public performance.

The first great name in 16th-century Venetian music is that of Adrian Willaert (*c.* 1490–1562), a great Flemish master who studied in Paris, joined the court at Ferrara in 1522, then came to Venice as *maestro di cappella* at San Marco in 1527 and lived there the rest of his long life. He brought to Italy all the new forms of northern European music, including the intricate music of his native land: in 1520 he published in Venice, 'French chansons in double canon', and he effected a brilliant combination of northern intellect and Italianate subtlety. He composed a very large collection of motets and some masses. In eight psalm settings he uses the San Marco *cori spezzati* – antiphonal choirs. As a teacher he gathered a group of faithful followers who, with their teacher, quite simply established the supremacy of Venice in composition and, equally important, in performance. The stage was set for greatness.

Music was one of the attainments of a gentleman. 'Musicke', wrote Castiglione in his Book of the Courtier, *'doth not onely make sweete the mindes of men, but also many times wilde beasts tame; and who so savoureth it not, a man may assuredly thinke him to be not well in his wits.'*
BELOW *portrait of a young man with a lute, by Giovanni Capriani.* BELOW LEFT *lute music printed in Venice in 1508, a very early example of tablature printed from type by double impression.*

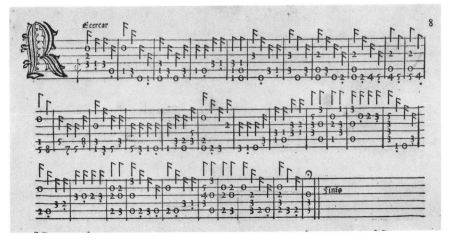

Contact between Venice and Germany existed at many levels, commercial and artistic. TOP *drawing of a Venetian woman made by Dürer during one of his stays in the city.* BELOW *office of the Augsburg financier Jacob Fugger, showing folders of letters from different cities: second from the top on the left is 'Venedig'.*

Andrea Gabrieli was born about 1515 in the unfashionable Venetian suburb of Canareggio; he is said to have come from a very minor branch of a noble family. In any case he was soon engaged as a singer at San Marco and later organist in the parish church of San Geremia. The crucial event in his life was that about 1560 he was called to the distinguished court of Duke Albrecht of Bavaria in Munich. In 1562 he accompanied the Duke to Nuremberg, Prague, Bamberg, Würzburg and Frankfurt-am-Main, where he participated in the ceremonies whereby Emperor Ferdinand obtained for his son Maximilian the title of King of the Romans.

His stay in Germany proved of vital importance for two reasons. Firstly, it provided a link between Germany and the Serenissima on a musical level. In Venice, there had always been cordial and reciprocal business relations between the two countries, as the famous district of Venice near the Rialto Bridge, the Fondaco dei Tedeschi (i.e. of the Germans), suggests. Now these relations were cemented further on a musical level, and the exchange of ideas was to continue when Andrea's nephew, Giovanni, went to Germany and when eminent German composers such as Hans Leo Hassler and Heinrich Schütz studied with Giovanni.

Secondly, the Bavarian court, with its sophisticated, worldly atmosphere had a fine orchestra and choir of some thirty-five musicians from all over Europe, some celebrated virtuosi, and some composers, of whom the most celebrated was Lassus, Orlando di Lasso, who was some seventeen years Gabrieli's junior but already a polished, sophisticated man who could compose in every genre.

Andrea Gabrieli learned much from Lassus. On his return to Venice in 1564 he was engaged as organist at San Marco. He embarked upon the same path as Lassus. He too showed that he could excel in all known musical genres. His first publication was a set of *Cantiones Sacrae*, sacred songs, dedicated to Duke Albrecht, modelled on a similar publication by Lassus a few years before.

Gabrieli was perhaps less profound than Lassus, and sought to be a bright, optimistic composer. He wrote dialect songs in the same vein of caricature as Lassus', and he had the same sensitivity to setting words to music, but he lacked Lassus' taste in poetry and he did not have the same academic interest in *musica reservata*. Essentially he aimed to entertain the widest possible audience rather than seeking to please the connoisseurs.

His madrigals went through edition after edition. His first published work in the genre was a madrigal 'Felici d'Adria', probably composed for the visit of the Archduke Charles of Carinthia in 1567. It was a work for eight voices and very much in the manner of Lassus, making use of exciting rhythms, simple harmony and complicated counterpoint.

His ceremonial church music set a new standard in the use of massed choirs and instruments, which was beyond the capacities of his superiors, Gioseffo Zarlini or his colleague Claudio Merulo. Andrea's motets began to show a richness of tone and quality hitherto unknown. Some are in the Lassus manner,

written for eight or more contrapuntal strands but with richer harmony and the lower registers, supported by the trombonist, exploited more fully.

The size of the San Marco choir did not allow for grand forces so Andrea gradually caused the San Marco *cappella* to be enlarged on the lines of the Munich forces. Andrea may largely have been responsible for the decision to take on a full-time instrumental ensemble in 1568. In 1585, a year before his death, he produced an astonishing tour-de-force: a sixteen-part Gloria with four separate choirs, performed at High Mass on the occasion of a state visit by Japanese princes.

Andrea's published instrumental music (*Ricercari e Madrigali*, collected by Giovanni and published in 1589) consists of pieces for four instruments, ideal for the San Marco ensemble.

We are not sure when and where Giovanni Gabrieli was born – it is thought in Venice about the year 1555. He was in any case the star pupil of his uncle, who treated him like the son he never had:

If Messer Andrea Gabrieli (of blessed memory) had not been my uncle, I should dare to say (without fear of being accused of bias) that, as there are few illustrious painters and sculptors gathered together in the world, so are there few indeed composers and organists as excellent as he is. But since by my consanguinity I am scarcely less than his son, it is not fitting for me to say freely that which affection, guided by truth, would seem appropriate to me.[10]

We are able to see how Andrea went about teaching from a document written by another of Andrea's pupils, Ludovico Zacconi, who was studying with the great organist and composer about 1577:

Andrea Gabrieli's works were collected by his nephew Giovanni and published three years after his death, in 1589 (ABOVE LEFT). After singing in the San Marco choir, Andrea began his career as organist at S. Geremia (ABOVE) and spent four years in Germany before taking up the post of organist at San Marco.

In 1597 Doge Marino Grimani (RIGHT) presided over the coronation of his wife as Dogaressa. Like most Venetian state occasions, it involved a procession and music – by Gabrieli. There are drummers to the left of the campanile and trumpeters to the right. On the extreme left can be seen the temporary triumphal arch built to receive the Dogaressa when she landed at the Piazzetta. The painting is by Andrea Michieli, called Vicentino.

Among the many pupils (among whom I number myself) of Sig. Andrea Gabrieli, most honoured organist of San Marco, there was one whom I will not name who had made many counterpoints upon a canto fermo, and being tired of it, asked the master whether he could change it; and the master looking at him with displeasure [this pupil] said 'Please, master, let me change this canto fermo, for I do not know what more I can do with it', and taking up a pen he (Gabrieli) composed four or five fughe, each one more beautiful than the other, and said 'Do you really think you had done everything possible . . .?'[11]

Obviously at the advice of, and with recommendations from, his uncle, Giovanni followed the trail to Munich. Lassus was in Venice in 1574 and seems to have taken on the young nephew of his friend, for by 1575 he was in Munich at the Bavarian Court – thus escaping the plague in Venice. Just as the orchestra and choir of San Marco had grown in the past decades, Munich now boasted sixty musicians with composers of talent among them – Giuseppe Guami, who was later in Venice, is the best known. There was a virtuoso cornet player named Francesco Laudis. And above all there was the great Lassus, who taught him the deceptively complex side of music that perhaps his uncle was inclined to overlook. Giovanni made friends in the several years he was in Germany – with the Fuggers, the great banker family to whom he dedicated later publications; the Bishop of Bamberg; a certain Georg Gruber, in charge of a confraternity that supplied music to the Frauenkirche in Nuremberg; and with the Abbot of SS. Afra and Ulrich in Augsburg. In turn, these men obviously admired and liked Giovanni and later sent their pupils and budding musicians to Venice to study with him.

Again like his uncle, Giovanni returned to Venice about 1584. There was then the dramatic moment when the organist at San Marco, Merulo, resigned to

go to Parma. There was an open competition for his successor which was set for New Year's Day 1585. This is what the document says in which it is stated that Gabrieli won, as it were, hands down:

> ... it being necessary to elect a new organist, the Procurators of San Marco, meeting in the sacristy to make the said election, by the method of secret ballot, which when opened, showed a unanimous vote in favour of the said Zuane Gabrieli who, on this decision being announced, came into the presence of the Illustrious Signori, thanking them deeply and promising to give every attention and care to his office.[12]

The procurators needed a composer of fluency, grandeur and reliability, for the previous *maestro di cappella*, Zarlino, had been an ageing one. He had been in their service for some forty years and in charge of the establishment for twenty. He had never been much of a composer, but he was undoubtedly one of the most learned men of his time (both as a theologian and as a musician).

His period of office had been efficient and peaceful. The cappella had become much larger and some notable musicians had been recruited, but there had been no great innovations.

Giovanni now proceeded to unfold a talent of prodigious span. He served three Doges: Pasquale Cicogna, Leonardo Donato and Marino Grimani. Grimani, Doge from 1595 to 1605, was musical and fond of ceremonial. His reign was rich in spectacular festivals and processions; in 1596 there was a splendid reception for the Duke and Duchess of Mantua; in 1597 he had his wife crowned as Dogaressa; in 1598 there were celebrations in honour of the peace between France and Spain; and pastoral plays in the Palazzo Ducale flourished as never before, with three performances each year.

It is not difficult to imagine the difference such a leader must have made to the

QVINTVS
SACRAE
SYMPHONIAE.
IOANNIS GABRIELII.
SERENISS. REIP. VENETIAR. ORGANISTÆ
IN ECCLESIA DIVI MARCI.
Ɓcnis, 7, 8, 10, 11, 14, 15, & 16, Tam
vocibus, Quam Inſtrumentis.
Editio Noua.
CVM PRIVILEGIO.

VENETIIS, Apud Angelum Gardanum.
M. D. XCVII.

Gabrieli's Sacrae
Symphoniae, *published in
Venice in 1598, broke new
ground in using three or four
groups of musicians —
arrangements that grew out of
the composer's work at San
Marco using two choirs.*

musicians of his chapel. The frequent opportunities to use them enabled the composer to gain experience in exploiting them. The result of this experience was two volumes of Gabrieli's 'Sacrae Symphoniae', works which extend the use of double choir to compositions for three or even four groups of musicians. Most of the surviving pieces are Mass movements, Magnificats, or settings of verses from some psalm or rejoicing which would do for any regal occasion. Any motets with texts relating specifically to an event would have been of little permanent value to the publisher.

In his large-scale church music, Giovanni strikes an extraordinary note, a combination of great grandeur and devotion, the multi-choired effects linked to music of rhapsodic power. This kind of music is brilliantly set forth in a very late work, *In Ecclesiis*, for three choirs – music of prophetic significance, looking forward to Bach.

The division into two choirs was the starting point for even more daring ventures. There was some tradition of adding a third choir by Giovanni's time. Willaert, Merulo and Andrea Gabrieli had all tried their hand at it during their respective careers. The problem was where to put the third choir and in 1586 a new platform with a third organ was added.

The main difference with three choirs was one of size and colour. Not much more could be done in the way of dialogue than was possible with two choirs. The gain comes in the sheer weight which the additional singers and players can bring and the greater sophistication of contrasting timbres which they make possible. The difference between the two choirs had been gradually growing from the 1560s onwards and the introduction of a third allowed a considerable expansion of such contrasts. The two choirs above could be pitted against the one below, the tutti against any one of the three, or one high and one low against the third on the other side of the altar, or a single choir could emerge magically from the tutti.

With three choirs it was possible to have twelve distinct melodic strands. Doubling the bass lines of the various choirs was a great convenience to the composer; it also made it less difficult to keep the counterpoint of the lines independent of one another. One way of easing the problem a little further was to expand the tonal range.

Giovanni Gabrieli's early motets for a single choir are marked by their relative simplicity, the extension of sonorities and the intelligibility of the text. He published two volumes of his and Andrea's motets in 1587 and 1597.

The major differences between Andrea's and Giovanni's Masses are differences of degree. Like his uncle, Gabrieli accepted the convention of contrast between choirs without too much change, and his motets are all written in conservative time values. But Giovanni uses a far wider harmonic range and shows greater flexibility within his time values. Also, Gabrieli the younger was much more aware of the religious needs of the text than his uncle. He had greater sensitivity to shades of mood and a distinctly original gift for melody.

In his double-choir motets he shows considerable skill, using great expressive power with a wider range of emotion than appears on the surface. Its scale may preclude intimacy, but not personal feelings. Gabrieli makes the techniques of the double choir an integral part of his conception.

Marietta Robusti, Tintoretto's daughter, was an accomplished artist (this is a self-portrait) and also evidently a musician.

Giovanni was also a skilled organist and a brilliant composer of music for organ. A pupil of his uncle and the great Merulo, his compositions fall into the same three categories of genre used by Andrea and Merulo: improvisatory music for toccatas and *intonazioni*; transcriptions and the imitation of transcriptions usually called 'canzona'; and the 'learned' piece, entitled '*ricercar*' or even '*fuga*'.

Improvisation was perhaps more common in 16th-century music than playing from the written notes. The greater part of teaching was done by means of extempore invention. The toccata of the Venetian organists is a sort of 'frozen improvisation'. Merulo and the two Gabrielis gave birth to the basic idea of the toccata as a piece which ranges from ricercar-like counterpoint to florid fingerwork.

Andrea's and Giovanni's compositions contain no 'romantic' elements, as Merulo's did. They are at times witty, usually extrovert and always well crafted but they lack spontaneity, unpredictability and sentimentality, though these were becoming fashionable.

Historically the organ compositions of the two Gabrielis had little influence on organ music elsewhere, and Giovanni was the last of Venice's great organists. But their compositions were some of the first organ pieces effectively to transfer a sophisticated vocal idiom into true keyboard music.

Even if none of the scores had survived from the 16th century, the world of Venetian music would be vividly evoked in paintings, though these are often idealized and allegorical rather than realistic. Tintoretto's Concert of Women *is a Parnassian vision of the power and beauty of music. But it is also a reminder that a great deal of music in Venice was indeed made by women.*

QVINTO
CONCERTI
DI ANDREA,
ET DI GIO: GABRIELI
ORGANISTI
DELLA SERENISS. SIG. DI VENETIA.

Continenti Musica DI CHIESA, Madrigali,
& altro, per voci, & ftromenti Musi-
cali; à 6. 7. 8. 10. 12. & 16.

Nouamente con ogni diligentia dati in luce.

LIBRO PRIMO ET SECONDO.
CON PRIVILEGIO.

IN VENETIA.
Appreffo Angelo Gardano. 1587.

LEFT Venus and the Organ-player *by Titian is a similarly stylized and intellectualized comment on the connection between music and love.*
ABOVE RIGHT Five Concerti *by Andrea and Giovanni Gabrieli, published in 1587.*
RIGHT *another painting from Titian's circle shows a scene much closer to ordinary life, with four men gathered round a musical score.*

Giovanni is, however, principally celebrated for his instrumental music, written for all sorts of combinations – grave Renaissance offerings with those dark-hued overtones that became so much a part of his style.

In the years just before Giovanni's appointment to the basilica, the ensemble was expanded. Instrumentalists were now considered of some importance. There were six players on the permanent staff, in addition to which the Treasurer was allowed to co-opt others if and when the occasion warranted.

Giovanni's close relationship to Giovanni Bassano and Girolamo Dalla Casa, the Maestro di Concerto, increased his own incentive to develop instrumental techniques. His music included methods of applying 'divisions' to a melodic line and written out ornaments and showed a natural tendency to embellish a scale, which resulted in the use of constant semiquaver patterns giving a regularity and order in rhythms. He tended to embellish a single line throughout a piece rather than sharing the ornamentation out equally among the parts.

Gabrieli's instrumental works were a beginning from which a new idiom emerged. Specific instruments were indicated for specific parts. He was the first to use the word 'sonata'. Little is left of the canzona's vocal origins. Without words, new patterns had to be invented which would make instrumental music self-explanatory. This had been done for the organ and lute by its virtuosi. Gabrieli did the same for the ensemble. He was not so much the originator of the sonata as the climactic figure in the story of the canzona.

Gabrieli's preference lay in the main for church music but he could not avoid the composition of secular music: from the mid-century, Venetian composers had written madrigals in praise of Venice for occasions when some spectacular procession outside San Marco needed a frankly patriotic chorus to stir the populace. For example, the Ascension Day crossing of the Bucintoro to the Lido was accompanied by the choir singing 'Epithalamiums' all the way. No music of this kind by Giovanni has come down to us, but there was one further occasion when official secular music was a *sine qua non*, and that was the pastoral play given in the courtyard of the Doge's Palace several times a year. There are some plays dating from the 1580s when Doges Da Ponte and Cicogna had a taste for them, but the bulk came from Marino Grimani's reign, the decade from 1595. Most of the music for these pastorals is lost. Unlike motets it could never be used again, since at the next festival there would be a completely new play. But what may have been Gabrieli's first official secular work for his Doge does survive – a piece written to accompany a play given in front of Doge Pasquale Cicogna on the Day of St Stephen 1585.

Over a dozen of Giovanni's madrigals were published during his first six years as organist at San Marco. He included six in his uncle's *Il terzo libro de madrigali a cinque voci* (1590); they all suggest that he was fully acquainted with the fashion of the 1580s. They are clearly, however, the work of a church musician or organist, not of an academician or courtier. Gabrieli's last known secular compositions are the 'Scherza Amarilli' written for a wedding in 1600 and 'Le Nozze di Hadriana' written for the entertainment given on St Stephen's Day 1600.

On 12 August 1612 Giovanni Gabrieli, Venice's greatest composer up to this time, died from a kidney stone.

II   The Seventeenth Century

The 17th century began for Venice with a major diplomatic triumph. She defied the Pope — and won. For long she had been famed for her religious toleration, welcoming Muslims and Jews (so long as the latter lived in the Ghetto reserved for them) and, in more recent years, all the various Protestant sects spawned by the Reformation; by 1600, however — largely as a result of the Edict of Nantes two years before, by which Henri IV granted his Protestant subjects freedom of worship and equal political rights with Catholics — her enlightened policies came under increasingly heavy fire from Rome, and with the accession of the Borghese Pope Paul V in 1605 her relations with the Papacy reached breaking point. Finally, in May of the following year, the ban of the Church was passed upon her.

Until that time, even the threat of interdict had been the most dreaded weapon in the papal armoury, one that had regularly brought kings and emperors to their knees; Venice herself had suffered three previous sentences — in 1284, 1309 and 1483 — each of which had cost her dear. This time, however, she simply ignored it. A decree signed by Doge Leonardo Donà instructed the clergy to continue as before with the cure of souls and the celebration of the Mass, and dismissed the Papal Nuncio.

Meanwhile, Venice fought back, championed by one of the most remarkable men in all her history. Legist and theologian, dialectician and political philosopher, polemicist and propagandist of genius, the Servite monk Paolo Sarpi worked untiringly to make the Republic's case understood throughout Europe. Thanks to his brilliant advocacy, England and Holland rallied to her support; Henri IV offered to mediate. Suddenly, the Pope and his Curia saw that their interdict had failed; worse, its failure had been revealed to the world. It must be lifted, and quickly. Venice drove a hard bargain, but he was in no position to make better terms. And so, in April 1607, after a little less than a year, the ban was lifted. It proved the last in the history of the Church.

Six months later, as he was returning from the Doge's Palace to his monastery, Sarpi was set upon by a gang of would-be assassins, stabbed three times and left for dead. Miraculously, he recovered; later, being shown the weapon, he tested its point and murmured punningly that he recognized the style of the Roman Curia. He was almost certainly right — a fact which seems in no way less shocking but perhaps somewhat less surprising when we remember that the 17th century, throughout most of Western Europe, was the Age of Intrigue. This was, admittedly, nothing new: in the Florence of the Medici and the Milan of the Visconti, above all in the Rome of the Borgias, there had been conspiracies and poisonings aplenty. Nor was it confined to Italy: many a Frenchman could remember the massacre of St Bartholomew and many an Englishman looked back with a shudder on the endless machinations surrounding the unhappy life of Mary Queen of Scots, while the first ten years

15 *Claudio Monteverdi in old age. Domenico Fetti's portrait movingly conveys the old man's magisterial authority and intellectual power. He is holding a Roman tragic mask, an allusion to his status as a dramatic artist ranking with the great classical writers.*

of the century saw both the assassination of Henri IV and the Gunpowder Plot. But it was above all in 17th-century Italy that it became a way of life – and Venice was no exception.

By now, thanks to her superb communications and the almost legendary stability of her government, the Most Serene Republic had become the espionage capital of Europe, numbering among her foreign residents agents of all the chief nations of the world. The greatest spymaster of all was, however, Venice herself. With an intelligence system of her own infinitely more highly developed than that of any foreign power, she kept a close eye on all these covert activities and, where possible, turned them to her own advantage – never more successfully than in uncovering what was known as the Spanish Conspiracy of 1618, by which the Duke of Osuna, Spanish Viceroy of Naples, planned to seize the city for himself, while all the leading Venetian nobles were seized or held to ransom.

Thus, by the time the century was a quarter through its course, Venice had averted two potential disasters. With the third, she was less lucky. In 1630 she was stricken by the plague, and sixteen months later had lost over 46,000 of her citizens – almost a third of her population which, now reduced to 102,000, was smaller than at any time since the 15th century. As a thank-offering after the former visitation of 1575, the survivors had built the church of the Redentore; on this occasion they decided to raise a still grander edifice at the entrance to the Grand Canal and to name it after the Blessed Virgin who, they hoped, would bring them both health and salvation: S. Maria della Salute. The architect chosen was the thirty-two-year-old Baldassare Longhena. The foundation stone was laid on 1 April 1631.

The last day of that same month was to prove fateful for the Republic, since it saw the departure from Constantinople of a Turkish fleet of 400 sail, carrying some 50,000 fighting men and bound for Crete, which as long ago as 1211 had become the first properly constituted Venetian colony and was now the last remaining in the Eastern Mediterranean. The Venetians defended their island heroically – its capital, Candia (now Heraklion) sustaining a twenty-two-year siege before the Captain-General, Francesco Morosini, negotiated an honourable surrender in 1669. Fifteen years later Morosini, now sixty-four, embarked on a new and remarkably successful campaign which was to regain Attica, the Peloponnese and many of the surrounding islands (blowing up the Parthenon in the process). In 1688 he was elected Doge – the last to lead an army in battle – and was still fighting when he died five years later. Fortunately he did not live to see the bulk of his conquests returned to the Sultan by the Treaty of Karlowitz in 1699.

An account of the arts during the period will not detain us long. Baldassare Longhena was the only great visual artist of 17th-century Venice. He certainly had nothing to fear from Giuseppe Sardi, the front of whose S. Maria del Giglio aroused the wrath of Ruskin for possessing not a single religious feature; and still less from the ridiculously-named Paduan Alessandro Tremignon, whose S. Moisè presents what is arguably the most hideous façade in all Venice. In painting and sculpture, too, it was as if the Venetians were exhausted by their astonishing performance in the seicento. Of those who worked regularly in the city the two most gifted, Domenico Tintoretto and Palma Giovane, were both formed in the earlier century; their nearest rivals, Vicentino and l'Aliense, would be forgotten were it not for their huge canvases in the Doge's Palace. There remains Sebastiano Ricci; but his earliest work in Venice (at S. Marziale) dates only from 1700. Altogether the overall vision we have of the city at this period is strangely monochrome – a black-and-white engraving rather than the blaze of light and colour that had gone before.

16   BELOW *a ceremony inside San Marco in the 17th century. It takes place at the high altar, in the choir behind the marble screen. Musical interest centres on the top right-hand corner, where instrumentalists are placed in a high gallery. There would be another group matching them on the other side.*

17   *Joseph Heintz's picture of the Piazza San Marco* (RIGHT) *in the 17th century includes a number of communal events that used to take place there, though it is perhaps too much to believe that they would all be happening together. On the left spectators cluster round a stage. On the right* commedia dell' arte *characters perform. In the middle there is bull-baiting and one bull seems even to have escaped.*

18   Joseph Heintz's second great Venetian picture shows the ceremony in which the Doge
crossed the bridge of boats to the Redentore on the Giudecca, to give thanks every year for
Venice's recovery from the plague. The head of the procession is already entering the church.

19 *Willem von Aelst's picture* The Concert
(LEFT) *might almost be an allegory of the senses,
combining the pleasures of music, of eating and
contemplating the beauty of women. Flautist and
lutenist concentrate on the same music book as they
play their duet.*
20 *Oboe, flute, violin and two lutes are present in
this musical still-life by Baschenis. A book of music
peeps out in the bottom right-hand corner.*

21 *One of the leading composers of 17th-century
Venice was a woman, Barbara Strozzi* (RIGHT), *the
illegitimate daughter of Giulio Strozzi, a patron of
Monteverdi. She was as talented as she was beautiful,
studying music with Cavalli and belonging to one of
the Venetian academies.*

22 *To Heinrich Schütz Giovanni Gabrieli repaid
the musical debt that he had incurred by studying in
Germany under Lassus. Schütz was Gabrieli's star
pupil in Venice and lived long enough to fall under the
spell of Monteverdi. The portrait is by Rembrandt.*

For Venice the 17th century began sensationally: the excommunication of the entire Venetian Republic!

Relations between Venice and Rome had been strained for some time – Rome had been trying to tighten its hold over La Serenissima, with little success. In 1605 a new Pope, Paul V, decided to take radical action. An ultimatum was issued to the Republic on Christmas morning, stating that if Venice failed to comply with certain of Rome's requirements, the Vatican would have no choice but to excommunicate the Republic.

La Serenissima's reaction was typical of her attitude towards Rome. In a document sent to all the patriarchs, archbishops, bishops, vicars, abbots and priors throughout the entire Venetian territories, the Doge of Venice on that fateful 6 May 1606 himself took what was nearly a heretic stance: he recognized in matters temporal no superior power except the Divine Majesty. The Doge then banned the Jesuits, the Theatines and Capuchins from all Venetian territory and dismissed the Papal Nuncio.

'We ignore your excommunication: it is nothing to us. Think now where this resolution would lead, if our example were to be followed by others,' wrote the Doge in his famous dismissal to the Papal Nuncio.[1] This was the greatest scandal of its time. There had been interdicts against Venice before: in 1284, 1309 and 1483 – but they had remained local. The excommunication of 1605 created resounding echoes throughout the Christian West. For the Vatican, the horror was that many Christian communities sided with La Serenissima. Spain was utterly hostile, but England and Holland both offered help. The Vatican had to face a dreadful reality: the interdict had failed, and as long as it remained in force the dread power of the Curia and the Pope was being challenged with ever increasing effect.

The Vatican was forced to accept an offer from France to mediate, and to accept Venice's choice of representative in the negotiations. Venice chose Paolo Sarpi, a Servite monk whose relations with Rome were, if possible, worse than the Republic's. Sarpi proved a brilliant and tough negotiator. The interdict was lifted in April 1607 but Venice did not re-admit the Jesuits.

Never again would the Vatican attempt such an excommunication. Times had changed; no longer was it possible for an excommunication to bring emperors and kings to their knees. In the manner of vengeful Renaissance princes, Pope Paul V engaged assassins to murder Paolo Sarpi. On 25 October 1607, he was set upon and stabbed three times whilst making his way from the Servite Monastery to the Doge's palace. Miraculously he survived this and two other attempts on his life, finally dying peacefully in his bed in 1623.

The high point in Venice's relations with the papacy had come in 1177, when Pope Alexander III visited the city and (according to popular belief) handed Doge Ziani a sword symbolizing his authority: an occasion remembered and optimistically commemorated by this painting in the Ducal Palace at the very time when relations between the two powers were at their worst.

Crete was Venice's bulwark against the Turks, who besieged it for twenty years before forcing it to surrender in 1669. The commander then was Francesco Morosoni (later Doge). In spite of some wishful pictures of his forces defeating the Turks (ABOVE), there was never any real hope of winning.

The rest of the century failed to live up to this impressive beginning. In 1630 Venice became involved in a war of succession. The Duke of Mantua had died, leaving his Duchy to Charles of Nevers, one of his French cousins. The Emperor, however, anxious to prevent the French from winning a foothold in Italy, advanced a rival claimant. Venice, equally anxious to keep the Emperor out of Italy, came to the aid of Nevers. The result was unedifying. The combined Venetian and Mantuan forces were routed and the Imperial troops sacked Mantua in 1630. A year later the Emperor needed his troops in Germany – peace was made and Nevers was reinstated. But the army had brought with it the plague to Italy. From 1631 to 1633 the Black Death raged in Venice, taking its toll from all levels of society. Venice lost some 46,500 citizens, reducing the population to its lowest level since the 15th century.

A period of peace followed, but 1645 found the Republic once again at war, this time with the Ottoman Empire. Twenty-four years of naval and military clashes, during which the fates favoured first one then the other side, finally terminated in 1669 with the fall of Crete, La Serenissima's most treasured colony, to the Turks. The Republic was on the verge of bankruptcy and had to concede defeat.

She also had to concede that the days in which she could sustain a prolonged state of warfare single-handedly against a major naval power were long gone by. The end of the century saw the Republic once more at war with the Turk, but this time almost as the sidekick to Austria, the main protagonist. Venice did not take the main brunt of the fighting, but neither did she take the lion's share of the spoils.

Yet the great Venetian Republic was by no means a spent force. Her super-efficient secret police had won for her a new role as the world centre of espionage, for which the growing 'tourist' trade to Venice was a good cover. The fame of La Serenissima's great beauty was spreading, and, with the gradual reduction of warfare in Europe, more and more people were beginning to travel for the sake of travel. Where better to go than Venice, that strange, exotic city on water, in which the grandeur of Byzantium and the soaring beauty of Renaissance Europe met in one glorious whole?

Venice had many wares to offer the adventurous traveller. He could sample the delights of Venetian women; there were no less than 20,000 courtesans in Venice at the beginning of the century, and they were quick to attract the attention of newcomers to the city. Thomas Nashe relates:

We made a long stride and got to Venice in short time; where having scarce lookt about us, a precious supernaturall pandor, apparelled in all points like a gentleman & having half a dosen several languages in his purse, entertained us in our owne tongue very paraphrastically and eloquently, & maugre all other pretended acquaintance, would haue us in a violent kinde of curtesie to be the guestes of his appointment. His name was Petro de campo Frego, a notable practitioner in the pollicie of baudrie. The place whether he brought us was a pernicious curtizas house named Tabitha the Temptresses, a wench that could set as civill a face on it as chastities first martyr Lucrecia. What will you conceit to be in any saints house that was there to seeke? Bookes, pictures, beades, crucifixes, why, there was a haberdashers shop of them in every chamber. I warrant you should not see one set of her neckercher perverted or turned awrie, not a piece of haire

displast. On her beds there was not a wrinkle of any wallowing to be found, her pillows bare out as smooth as a groning wives belly, & yet she was a Turke and an infidel, & had more dooings then all her neighbours besides. Us for our money they used like Emperours.[2]

Another source of pleasure was the Carnival, a series of revels and processions during which all Venice became giddy with self-indulgence. John Evelyn describes the 1640 Carnival in his diary as follows:

The Women, Men & persons of all Conditions disguising themselves in antique dresses & extravagant Musique & a thousand gambols, & traversing the streetes from house to house, all places then accessible, & free to enter: There is abroad nothing but flinging of Eggs fill'd with sweete Waters, & sometimes not over sweete; they also have a barbarous costume of hunting bulls about the Streetes & Piazzas, which is very dangerous, the passages being generally so narrow in that Citty: Likewise do the youth of the several Wards & parrishes contend in other Masteries or pastimes (fighting each other on the bridges) so as tis altogether impossible to recount the universal madnesse of this place during this time of licence: Now are the great banks set up for those who will play at Basset, the Comedians have also liberty & the Operas to Exercise: Witty pasquils are likewise thrown about, & the Mountebanks have their stages in every Corner: The diversion which chiefly tooke me up, was three noble Operas which I saw, where was incomparable Voices, & Musique.[3]

Between 1631 and 1633 bubonic plague swept through Venice, killing over 46,000 inhabitants. In an attempt to appease divine judgement, the Venetians vowed to build a church in honour of the Virgin. It was fifty years before it was finished, but S. Maria della Salute has taken its place among the great sights of Venice.

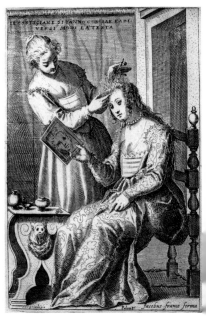

Music was everywhere in 17th-century Venice — on the canals, in the piazzas, in taverns and houses of ill-repute. Here one of the gondolas even has a harpsichord on board; on another an open-air supper is in progress. RIGHT a book published in 1609 shows the costume worn by courtesans, and the cortegiana principale is represented playing a keyboard instrument, possibly an organ.

LEFT a serenade. The lady looks out of the window. The lover sings, accompanying himself on the lute, backed by an ensemble of viols and virginals. RIGHT John Evelyn commented on the dangerous sport of allowing bulls to run free in the streets and public squares during Carnival time. More prudent spectators evidently preferred to watch from their windows.

Professional entertainers, including musicians, flourished in Venice as nowhere else. It was the birthplace of the commedia dell'arte, of the comedy of manners and of opera as public entertainment. LEFT a series of stages set up in the Piazza San Marco for various performers; once again, the musician is a woman.

This anonymous painting is tentatively identified as our earliest portrait of Monteverdi. He seems to be about thirty, when he would still have been at the Gonzaga court in Mantua. Invited to Venice in 1613, he was required to demonstrate his talents. On the morning of 19 April 1613, he rehearsed one of his compositions at S. Giorgio Maggiore (RIGHT), *and in the afternoon crossed the water to San Marco to play it there. He was appointed* maestro di cappella *that day.*

This extract was written just one year after Venice witnessed a revolution in the field of music; the world's first public performance of an opera. By 1640, as John Evelyn's diary shows, Opera was already a major part of life in Venice. Much of the history of music in Venice in the remainder of the 17th century is concerned with the rapid development and popularization of opera, a process which was spearheaded by the greatest Venetian composer of that century, Claudio Monteverdi.

On 10 July 1613 Giulio Cesare Martinengo, who had been in charge of music at San Marco, died. He had been ill for some time and under his inefficient and lax hand, standards had been lowered perilously; the choir was actually depleted. The procurators sent out requests to ambassadors and residents at Mantua, Milan, Padua, Bergamo, Brescia, Vicenza and even Rome for suggestions for a new *maestro di cappella*. One such document, dated 16 July, was sent to the Venetian resident at Milan. It says:

Since the death of our maestro di capella at our church of San Marco various people have been proposed, among others Signor Claudio Monteverdi . . . But we would be pleased to receive information concerning his worth and his ability . . .[4]

In the event the general opinion about Monteverdi was so favourable that the procurators invited him to come to Venice and display his talents with a composition. He rehearsed it at San Giorgio on 19 August 1613, in the morning. In the afternoon he played the work at San Marco. Monteverdi won the hearts of the procurators and was hired forthwith at a salary half as much again as that of his predecessor. They also gave him a handsome sum, 50 ducats, for travel expenses, with which he at once bought a serge coat.

Monteverdi's reputation had been built up under the Gonzagas, unworthy as they were of his genius. Their palace at Mantua (RIGHT), partly designed by Giulio Romano, was the setting for the first performance of many of his works, including the madrigals that were soon famous all over Italy. His First Book *was issued in Venice in 1607.*

On his return to Cremona he, his sons and his maidservant packed their belongings and returned to Venice, but en route were robbed on the road between Mantua and Este, at Sanguinetto. It was a carefully planned robbery and the Monteverdis lost almost all their worldly goods. It was a fitting end to what had been years of shameful treatment at the hands of the ruling Gonzaga family in Mantua.

Vincenzo Gonzaga had succeeded his father as Duke of Mantua in 1587. He embodied all the good and bad sides of the typical Renaissance ruler: he loved art, music and pageantry; and the court coffers which had been carefully filled by his father, emptied rapidly as Mantua witnessed what was to be a final golden harvest of splendour, culture and luxurious living. Vincenzo was a patron of Galileo and the young Rubens, and he freed the broken Torquato Tasso from prison and certain death. His amorous adventures and conquests were the scandal and (among courtiers) delight of Renaissance Europe. He engaged Monteverdi as a singer and player. The young Claudio, the son of a distinguished Cremonese physician, had, at the age of fifteen, published several sets of madrigals and canzonette. This is not as extraordinary as it may at first seem. Men and women grew up quickly in those days; women married at fifteen and at that age a composer would be *expected* to be able to write music. What is extraordinary, however, is that the music of the fifteen-year-old Monteverdi is so good.

Monteverdi seems to have joined the Gonzaga Cappella in about 1590. The history of his relationship to Duke Vincenzo is a very curious one: on the one hand the combination turned out to make musical and particularly operatic history; the Duke obviously liked him and took him along on various trips, including Hungary; but on the other hand Monteverdi was badly paid and often kept waiting months for his salary. Consider the following letter from Monteverdi to Vincenzo:

... This letter of mine has no other end than to come to your feet to ask Your Highness to give the order for my pay which is now five months in arrears, in which plight is also Signora Claudia, and my father-in-law, and the sum increases in this way so that I see no hope of having it in the future without a special order from Your Highness, without which all my labours will remain failing and ruinous since day by day I am running up debts and I cannot repay them.[5]

Claudio had been at Mantua for four or five years when he fell in love with Claudia Cattaneo, a beautiful young singer in the Duke's service, the daughter of a viola player in the court orchestra. They were married on 20 May 1599. Little is known of their relationship, but it is clear from their letters that he was devoted to her. Their free time was certainly spent (apart from running their little house) in music making and rehearsing, like the Bach family a century later.

In 1601 Benedetto Pallavicino, *maestro di cappella* at Mantua, died, but Vincenzo, who had rushed off again to Hungary to fight the Turks, made no move to advance Monteverdi. This was by no means the first time Monteverdi had been neglected in the matter of the appointment to this coveted post and Claudio's patience finally snapped. He wrote the Duke a famous and ironic letter in which he rather waspishly suggested that, after having been passed over so often, it 'would give rise to a scandal' if he were not made *maestro* of the Mantuan cappella.

... if, when the world has seen my zeal in Your Highness's service and your graciousness to me after the death of the most famous Signor Striggio, and after that of the excellent Signor Giaches (de Wert), and thirdly after that of the most excellent Signor Franceschino (Robigo) and finally after this the death of the capable Benedetto Pallavicino – if I failed to seek (on the grounds not of merit but of the faithful and singular devotion that I have always given in Your Highness's service) the ecclesiastical post now vacant, and if after all this I were not to ask with vigour and with humility for the said rank, it could be claimed with justice that I was negligent.[6]

The Duke seems to have been amused and granted Monteverdi's request.

L'ARTVSI

Ouero

DELLE IMPERFETTIONI
DELLA MODERNA MVSICA

Ragionamenti dui.

Ne' quali si ragiona di molte cose vtili, & necessarie alli Moderni Compositori.

DEL R. P. D. GIO. MARIA ARTVSI DA BOLOGNA.

Canonico Regolare nella Congregatione del Saluatore.

Nouamente Stampato.

In Venetia, Appresso Giacomo Vincenti, 1600.

STVDIOSI LETTORI.

Non vi marauigliate ch'io dia alle stampe questi Madrigali senza prima rispondere alle oppositioni, che fece l'Artusi contro alcune minime particelle d'essi, perche sendo io al seruigio di questa Serenissima Altezza di Mantoa non son patrone di quel tempo che tal'hora mi bisognarebbe: hò nondimeno scritta la risposta per far conoscere ch'io non faccio le mie cose à caso, & tosto che sia riscritta vscirà in luce portando in fronte il nome di SECONDA PRATICA, ouero PERFETTIONE DELLA MODERNA MVSICA, delche forse alcuni s'ammireranno non credendo che vi sia altra pratica, che l'insegnata dal Zerlino; ma siano sicuri, che intorno alle consonanze, & dissonanze, vi è anco vn'altra consideratione differente dalla determinata, la qual con quietanza della ragione, & del senso diffende il moderno comporre, & questo hò voluto dirui sì perche questa voce SECONDA PRATICA talhora non fosse occupata da altri, sì perche anco gli ingegnosi possino fra tanto considerare altre seconde cose intorno all'harmonia, & credere che il moderno Compositore fabrica sopra li fondamenti della verità. Viuete felici.

TAVOLA DELLI MADRIGALI:

Cruda Amarilli	1	Che dar più vi poss'io	13
O Mirtillo Mirtillo anima mia	2	M'è piu dolce il penar	14
Era l'anima mia	3	Ahi come a un vago sol	16
Ecco Siluio. Prima parte.	4	Troppo ben può	17
Ma se con la pietà. Secon.par.	5	Amor se giusto sei	19
Dorinda hà dirò. Terza par.	6	T'amo mia vita	20
Ecco piegando. Quarta par.	7	A sei voci.	
Ferir quel petto. vlt. par.	8	E così à poco à poco.	21
Ch'io t'ami. Prima parte.	10	A noue voci.	
Deh bella e cara. Secon.par.	11	Sinfonia. Questi vaghi.	22
Ma tu piu che mai. vlt. par.	12		

In 1600 a Bolognese musician, Giovanni Artusi — a sort of 17th-century Beckmesser — launched an attack on 'the imperfections of modern music', especially that of Monteverdi, for breaking the traditional Flemish rules of harmony and counterpoint. Monteverdi defended himself in the Preface to his Fifth Book of Madrigals (RIGHT), *concluding airily: 'I have not the time for an elaborate argument.'*

Monteverdi was by this time a very popular composer. His first three books of madrigals met with great enthusiasm from the public, although they were severely criticised by other musicians for their harmonic daring and for their supposed violation of the strict, old-fashioned rules. In the next years the Fourth (1603) and Fifth (1605) Books of Madrigals came into being, each one becoming more popular: the Fifth ran to no less than eight editions. Despite his *maestro di musica*'s fame, the Duke kept him at near-starvation wages, so that the Monteverdi family (there were two children by the time the Fifth Book of Madrigals was issued) had to receive substantial financial help from his father to keep alive. Gradually Claudia became weaker and weaker with a racking cough which would not go away; her husband was weighed down by overwork and pressing debts. Vincenzo, as he galloped across the darkened city to the latest of his voluptuous mistresses waiting for him in the Palazzo del Tè, wasted no more thought on his *maestro di musica* than on the debts piling up on the desk of the court treasurer.

Yet, with all these cares and worries Monteverdi was still able to create a work which would be one of the most significant in the history of music.

As the 1590s progressed, it was clear that a new and exciting period in music was beginning. In 1594, the two greatest musicians in Europe, Lassus and Palestrina, died within a few months of each other. The great age of polyphonic music was drawing to a close, making way for a new age of complex harmonies and richer textures. A new age which would give birth to an exciting and exotic musical experience: opera.

The Renaissance had turned back to ancient Greece and Rome for inspiration, and in Florence, a brilliant group of poets, intellectuals and

Monteverdi's Orfeo *was his first opera. Performed at Mantua in 1607, it was printed in 1615, but the score (*LEFT*) gives the basic melodic line only, with no clue as to the orchestration. The portrait dates from after his death.*

musicians were hard at work to invent a new musical genre wherein the old Greek tragedies and fables could be revived and clothed in modern garb. The 'Camerata', as the group called itself, invented the recitative, in which the words of the drama were closely matched to a sung, 'reciting' line, accompanied by a few instruments. During the years 1594–96, the new form was being examined, discussed and tried out: in 1597, the 'Camerata' was ready and *Dafne*, as the piece was entitled (music by J. Peri, text by O. Rinuccini), was performed during Carnival at the Palazzo Corsi in Florence. Opera was born. In the next few years, *Dafne* was repeated several times and improved.

Intellectuals throughout Italy were fascinated by the new form: the 'Camerata' continued to experiment, and in 1600 a second opera, *Euridice*, was produced: the text was again by Rinuccini and two composers set it to music: Peri and Caccini; Peri's version (which included bits of the Caccini) was given first, while Caccini's was staged two years later. The first performance of the Peri setting was given in honour of the marriage of Henry IV of France with Maria de' Medici, on 6 October 1600. A Mantuan singer sang the title role. Duke Vincenzo Gonzaga was invited to the nuptials, probably attended by Claudio Monteverdi, who had been in the Duke's entourage when they had visited Flanders the year before. We have no evidence of Monteverdi's reactions to *Euridice*: the agelessly beautiful subject obviously appealed to him, as we shall see; but what he thought of Peri's elegantly monotonous music with its thin accompaniment, we do not know. It does not perhaps exceed the bounds of scholarship, however, if we surmise that the experience of that October evening in 1600 planted the seed which was to bear fruit so brilliantly in Mantua a few years later.

Vincenzo's two sons, Francesco and Ferdinando, were also passionate addicts of the theatre. Ferdinando, studying at Pisa, seems to have followed avidly the activities of the Florentine 'Camerata'. Could not something of this sort be produced at Mantua? He and Monteverdi had long discussions; it seemed the natural thing to choose the story of Orpheus as the subject. One of the courtiers, A. Striggio, Jr. (whose father had been a celebrated musician at the Gonzaga court), fashioned the text. A hundred years after Andrea Mantegna's death (1506) perhaps the second most important work of art in the history of Mantua was born.

Monteverdi's *Favola d'Orfeo*, though of course owing its physical existence to the efforts of the Florentine 'Camerata', is a far cry from the earlier music of Peri and Caccini. When the thrilling trumpet toccata which opens *Orfeo* first sounded at Mantua on 22 February 1607, the cognoscenti (led by the Hereditary Prince Francesco) knew they were hearing a new kind of opera: instead of Peri's thin accompaniment of harpsichord and two or three strings, there was a rich and mighty orchestra, some forty strong; choruses delighted the ear and ballets the eye; Florentine recitative, Gabrieli-like intermediums for wind band, songful ariosos and madrigalian choral textures succeeded one another with breathtaking virtuosity. '*Orfeo*', writes the Monteverdi scholar H.F. Redlich, '. . . is really the first opera in

the sense of practical music-making; not simply the oldest operatic work certain to produce an immediate effect upon modern audiences; . . . Monteverdi's accomplishment . . . consists in the concentration of phenomena of style . . . into a complete image of sound, a musical cosmos which peers, Janus-like, into the past . . . as well as into the future of the Gluck-Wagnerian 'Birth of the drama from the spirit of music.[7]

Flushed with the triumph of *La Favola d'Orfeo*, Monteverdi was to have a bitter reward: on 10 August the tired and ageing master conducted a performance of the opera in Cremona, the town of his birth. A month later Claudia, who had accompanied him, died.

Monteverdi was on the edge of a nervous breakdown. Bitterly mourning the death of his wife and desperately short of money he was now faced with cuts in his salary from the Duke, who had unlimited money for his mistresses but apparently not enough for his musicians. The following poignant letter from the Town Musicians to the Duke illustrates how little consideration Vincenzo showed towards them.

A reminder to your Highness from the players who served you at the baptism at which there were seven festivals and seven days during which they had been in the service of Your Highness of Gonzaga, begging your Highness to give them satisfaction for they are poor men.[8]

Yet this neglect was not accompanied by any reduction in the Duke's demands to his employees. Keen to follow up the success of *Orfeo* with a whole series of operas, the Duke set Monteverdi to work on another opera, *Arianna*. Despite 'tremendous overwork . . . (and) headaches' Monteverdi rose to the challenge and when the opera was staged on 28 May 1608 at Mantua, the audience was moved to tears during the famous 'Lament'. A description of the first performance,

written by the official court chronicler survives in the Gonzaga Court Archives:

... Every part succeeded well, most especially miraculously the lament which Ariadne sings on the rock when she has been abandoned by Theseus, which was acted with much emotion and in so piteous a way that no one hearing it was left unmoved, nor among the ladies was there one who did not shed a few tears at her plaint.[9]

Monteverdi called this lament 'la più essential parte dell'opera'; but its survival does not lessen the tragic fact that the rest of the score is irrevocably lost.

As the next years came and went, the court began to owe Monteverdi considerable sums of money. Claudio's father even resorted to writing a letter to the Duchess Eleonora in the hope that she would intervene. It is a proud letter and a shame to the Gonzaga name: it opens:

Illustrious Lady, My son, Claudio Monteverdi, came to Cremona immediately after the end of the Wedding Festivities in a very bad state of health, in debt, and shabbily clad. Without any assistance from Signora Claudia he was now left, after her death, with the two poor children, who were a burden to him because his resources were only twenty scudi per month. I am absolutely certain that the trouble is due solely to the air of Mantua, which does not suit him, and to the exhausting work he has undertaken, and will continue to undertake, if he remains any longer in service. All this is combined with the misfortunes that have attended him throughout the nineteen years he has spent in the service of the illustrious Duke of Mantua. For this reason I have latterly decided to write to Your Highness and to beseech you most humbly in the name of Heaven to grant him the favour of release from his duties. For I am sure, noble Lady, that if he returns to

The most famous single piece of music by Monteverdi was an aria from his (otherwise lost) second opera Arianna. *The story is that of Ariadne, left abandoned by her lover Theseus on the island of Naxos. Her lament* Lasciatemi morire *('Let me die') conveyed emotion in a way that had never been heard in music before. Even this aria was almost lost to us — only two copies of the printed score survive.*

Mantua, the strenuous work and the unfavourable air will speedily be the cause of his death, and then these poor children will become a burden to me, who am old and frail, and who have, moreover, had in the past to maintain his wife, children, man-servants and maid-servants, and have not infrequently paid out 500 scudi on behalf of the said Claudio, and even larger sums when he was in His Highness' service in Hungary and Flanders, and again when he came to Cremona with his wife and children, a maid, servants and a carriage, and on other occasions which for the sake of brevity I will not mention. And as his wife received no reply to her appeal I have taken it upon myself to beseech Your Highness to beg of your illustrious consort that for God's sake he will grant me this just request; for it is certain that such a favour could only turn out to the said Claudio's advantage.[10]

In the midst of this financial misery and loneliness for his wife, the prematurely aged composer began in 1610 to write one of his loveliest and most moving compositions; the Vespers of the Blessed Virgin Mary. It is almost beyond human comprehension that at a time like this he could speak, as he does in the Sonata sopra Sancta Maria, a language of such utter purity and inner peace; in such moments as the 'great' (as opposed to the smaller) 'Magnificat septem vocibus et sex instrumentalis', wherein the searingly beautiful old plainchant floats through and over the rich tapestry of orchestral sound, Monteverdi gave his thoughtless patron a monument far greater than he deserved.

The end came quickly: the Duchess died unexpectedly in September 1611, to be followed in February of the next year by the profligate Duke. Francesco IV – who had helped to create Orfeo – mounted the Gonzaga throne; and showed his devotion to his maestro di musica by dismissing Monteverdi from the ducal service on the last day of July 1612, barely six weeks after he had become ruler of Mantua.

Broken-hearted, Monteverdi left Mantua a month later, carrying with him the sum of twenty-five scudi as a reward for twenty-one years of faithful service to the illustrious and noble house of Gonzaga.

From the time of his arrival in Venice, however, Monteverdi's life takes on a more serene aspect. Venice needed Monteverdi. Not only was the standard of the chapel musicians at San Marco alarmingly low, but the year before Monteverdi arrived in Venice, Giovanni Gabrieli, their doyen of composers had died (1612). The forces at San Marco numbered some thirty singers, including castrati, plus six instrumental players. Monteverdi set about reorganizing the choir and orchestra, bringing them up to strength.

Monteverdi's life was now a far happier one. His position was commensurate with his talents. It not only brought him a lot of money but it was also a dignified post, one which placed him on a high social level, unlike at Mantua where musicians were regarded as servants. It must have been a proud moment for him when he received this note by the Venetian procurators three years after his appointment at San Marco:

The procurators, knowing the work and efficiency of D. Claudio Monteverdi, maestro di cappella of San Marco, and wishing to confirm his appointment and give him the incentive to attend to the services of the Church to the honour of God with a whole heart, and in the desire that he will live and die in this service, have, by ballot, determined that he shall be confirmed in his post for ten years with a salary of 400 ducats per year with the usual perquisites.[11]

These perquisites included free lodging in a building which adjoined the Basilica; his apartment to be furnished according to the Maestro's wishes; and the usual allowance of wine. Not only was Monteverdi well provided for materially: he also had the satisfaction of knowing his work to be highly valued. 'Wherever I go to make music, whether it be chamber music or church music, the whole city is eager to be there. My duties are extremely agreeable.'[12]

Monteverdi's life in Venice was not without its difficulties, however. One drama – which might have ended stickily – was the arrest in Mantua of one of his sons by the Inquisition for having read a book on the forbidden list; but Claudio supported his son and was able to prove to the church authorities (with the aid of influential friends) that his son had read the book in all innocence.

Monteverdi wrote the following letter to Striggio in Mantua on 8 July 1628 in an attempt to gain his son's release:

I understand from your extremely kind letter that you have called personally on the worthy Pater Inquisitor, and I feel not a little embarrassed that you should have shown me this favour. Your Honour was told that the two days Massimiliano spent in captivity should suffice to restore him to absolute freedom. I doubt it, and Your Honour will excuse me if, in view of your own confidence, I speak so openly. I am afraid, and so is he – I mean, my son is afraid he will be put on the rack and condemned to pay an exceptional fine or to undergo imprisonment for infinitely more than two days; . . . Your Honour will believe me when I tell you that hardly a day passes that he does not weep or that he is not in the depths of despair. By the post which has lately arrived, the worthy Pater Inquisitor has written to me stating definitely that he will consent to letting me have my son back as soon as I wish. . . . Dear Sir, if only this great favour could be granted, may I beg you with all my heart and soul to obtain it for me? I assure you, life would thus be restored to myself and the lad, for this dread care is tormenting my spirit . . . [13]

His son was eventually released as requested.

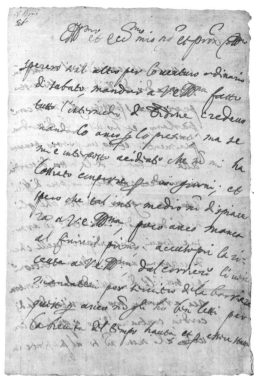

SERENISSIMA
SIGNORA
ET PATRONA COLLENDISSIMA.

ON Ardirei d'apprefentare quefto mio nuouo Concerto de Madrigali all'Altezza Voftra Sereniffima s'io non foffi ficuro, ch'ella
benche fia auezza à Concerti di Mufe Concertati dallo fteffo
Apollo, non fi fdegna però d'udire tal'hora qualche rozzo fuono
d'humil Sampogna, perche apparò fino nelle fafce, da fuoi
Gran Genitori à pregiare le cofe rare, & non ifpregiare le vili.
Quefti miei Componimenti (quali fi fiano) faranno publico, &
autentico teftimonio del mio diuoto affetto, verfo La Sereniffima
Cafa Gonzaga, dà me feruita con ogni fedeltà, per decine d'Anni;
Seruiramo per folenne preghiera, perche L'Autore fià ammeffo,
fe non frà piu degni, almeno frà piu fuifcerati ferui di V. A.
Sereniffima affine che poffa egli continuare per tutto'l corfo di fua vita, nella feruitù riuerente
già incominciata con la Sereniffima Madama Leonora di Feliciffima memoria ; per palefare al
Mondo le gratie Singolari, che tutto diuicene dal Sereniffimo Signor Duca Ferdinando di V. A.
Degniffimo Confort: & di lui fuo Singolar Signore, Cofi foffero le parole di quefte mie debolezze,
tante Lingue faconde, & tante penne eloquenti le note, che Celebraffero, in qualche parte le virtù
Heroiche dell'A. A. V: V. Sereniffime ; mà conofcendole io piu degne d'effere ammirate col'
filentio, che celebrate con parole, qui mi ammutolifco, & con quello fpirito ch'io poffo maggiore
prego loro dal Cielo il compimento d'ogni vera Felicità, & Humiliffimamente me L'inchine.

Di Venetia à di 13. Decembre   1619.

D. V. A. Sereniffima.

Humilliffimo & Deuotiffimo Seruitore

Claudio Monteuerde.

Monteverdi's life changed dramatically when he
left the service of the Gonzagas and became
maestro di cappella of San Marco. At
Mantua he had been dependent on court favours,
forced to solicit patronage by flattering
dedications such as that of his Sixth Book of
Madrigals (LEFT). Venice gave him security
and dignity, apparent in the portrait by Bernardo
Strozzi (ABOVE LEFT). A newly-discovered
letter (ABOVE and RIGHT), addressed to the
Marchese Enzo Bentivoglio in September 1627,
discusses the problems of setting to music a
libretto forming part of a wedding celebration at
Parma. There were arias for personifications of
the Months and for the goddess of Discord,
whom he proposes to make 'declaim without
music'. What he wrote does not survive.

che posso havere in riceuere gli detti
canti, per hauer a tempo obedito a
suoi comandi; perche qua in Venetia
si uociferra che tali uolte d'essi Ser.mi
Prencipi si debono fare il prossimo
uenturo Carneual del 1628, et qui faccendo
a V.ra humill.ma riuerenza a V.E. Ill.ma gli
bacio la mano. Da Venetia gli 19
9bris 1627

Di V.E. Ill.ma

Humill.mo et obblig.mo seru.re

Claudio monteuerdi

A further incident occurred to mar his happiness in Venice. In 1637 Monteverdi was forced to write to the Procurators of San Marco.

Yesterday morning before the great door of San Marco Domenico Aldegati, a singer at San Marco, . . . having respect neither for the office that I hold from the most serene Republic, nor for my age and my priesthood, but spurred on by a wild fury and with a loud raucous voice (and having brought together more than 50 people) spoke these exact words. 'The director of music belongs to a race of big cut-throats, a thieving, cheating, he-goat . . . I call him and whoever protects him an ass . . .'

I come therefore to your excellencies' feet not as Claudio Monteverdi the priest, for as such I shall forgive him; but as director of music whose authority derives from the Royal hand of the most serene Republic . . .[14]

He then threatens to resign if a similar event occurs. How seriously this threat should be taken is uncertain, as the position of *maestro di cappella* brought with it many benefits, as stated earlier. The necessity to resign seems not to have arisen, however, as Monteverdi continued as *maestro di cappella* until his retirement in 1643.

The authorities in Venice – unlike his princely employers in Mantua – allowed their *maestro di cappella* to compose sacred and secular music for others so long as it did not interfere with his heavy duties at San Marco. This outside work was a pleasant extra source of income. He was often asked to compose music for the ceremonies at S. Rocco and he was also befriended by many members of the rich and cultivated Venetian aristocracy.

He also found time to continue publishing his madrigals. Altogether his secular music was proving to be enormously successful. His madrigals, of which he published a total of nine extraordinary books, sometimes went through six editions, and his songs could be heard on a summer night floating over the canals. So celebrated were they all over Europe, that today copies may be found as far apart as York Minster, Breslau, Augsburg and Dubrovnik.

If one examines the list of music Monteverdi composed while in Venice, one's heart sinks at the number of lost masterpieces – a huge Requiem about which only a long description survives, (including the fact that the whole audience was moved to tears), half a dozen lost operas including *Arianna* (only one aria survives), Christmas masses – and some of it might be mouldering in one of the palazzi, or in the attics of the great villas along the Brenta.

The reason for these sad losses lies in the fact that relatively few of his works were published. Although very popular during his lifetime, his music went out of fashion soon after his death and few copies of his unprinted works have survived the long years of neglect which resulted. Those works which *have* survived were mostly published by Gardano, the famous Venetian music publisher. This firm published Monteverdi's first works, sacred songs for three voices, when he was fifteen; it also published Andrea and Giovanni Gabrieli and the first fruit of Heinrich Schütz. It is to them that we owe the only surviving extract (the Lament) from *Arianna*.

The head of the firm was Angelo Gardano, who lived from 1540 to 1611. After his death the firm was taken over by his son-in-law Bartolomeo Magni, to whom we owe Monteverdi's late works, especially the great collection of sacred music, *Selva morale e spirituale* of 1640, which gives us the Gloria from the music for the Plague and two dozen other masterpieces as well.

As Monteverdi was comfortably drifting into a serene old age, an event occurred which changed the history of music. In 1636 Francesco Manelli and Benedetto Ferrari, two Roman singers and opera composers, arrived in Venice. Monteverdi engaged them forthwith for the choir of San Marco. The next year Manelli persuaded the authorities to let him open a public opera house in Venice, San Cassiano.

San Cassiano was organized in such a way that the nobility could hire a box for the season and the citizens could purchase a ticket for the pit. So it was in fact the first public opera house. It was the beginning of one of the great innovations of the Baroque period – for opera rapidly became the rage of Western Europe. Soon there were opera houses from Lisbon to St Petersburg and from Louisiana to Vienna.

In 1639, when Monteverdi was seventy-two, the San Cassiano theatre revived *Arianna*. At the age of seventy-five he wrote perhaps his greatest opera: *L'incoronazione di Poppea* (the Coronation of Poppea).

It is extraordinary to think that this pious man, *maestro di cappella* of San Marco, could write the music to this worldly and licentious drama in which, as it were, villainy wins out completely (that is to say, Nero manages to get rid of his wife and to marry Poppea). The love duet at the end of the opera between Poppea and the Roman emperor, with its vicious cynicism, is astonishing; the victory of pure evil. There is something almost obscene about it, all the more so since the music which Monteverdi wrote is of a disarming simplicity and purity. And yet there are curiously ominous moments before. Arnalta, Poppea's nurse, who is devoted to her, sings a kind of lullaby, 'Adagiati, Poppea' which is full of foreboding, an extraordinarily moving interlude in the action, as it were.

In 1643 the composer made a farewell visit to Mantua, which had been sacked thirteen years before and was still in ruins. What must Monteverdi, now in priestly garb and nearing his eightieth birthday, have thought that summer morning as he surveyed the scene of his triumph and shame: the still blackened ruins where so many of his music pieces had perished; the half-empty Ducal Reggia, where he had begged for his salary; the swampy plains which had brought slow death to his beloved wife?

Claudio was now a very old man and in joining the church he had renounced the things of this world. But perhaps he dimly remembered with the indistinct mellowness of an octogenarian the splendid first performance of the *Favola d'Orfeo* – that memorable evening so long ago, when (and he might even have sensed this with the sure intuition of the genius) the course of Western music had been so swiftly and so magnificently altered.

Monteverdi died on 29 November 1643, deeply mourned by the whole of Venice:

. . . The news of such a loss upset and turned all the city to sadness and mourning, and was accompanied, not by singing from the choir of singers of San Marco, but by their tears and weeping.[15]

Foremost of Venetian music publishers in the 17th century were Angelo Gardano and Bartolomeo Magni. Their edition of Monteverdi's sacred music, Selva Morale e Spirituale *was printed in 1640.*

VERDE ✶ CLAVDIO MONTE

FIORI POETICI
Raccolti nel Funerale
DEL MOLTO ILLVSTRE,
E Molto Reuerendo
SIGNOR CLAVDIO
Monte verde
Maeſtro di Cappella della Du-
cale di S. Marco.
Conſecrati
DA D. GIO: BATTISTA
Marinoni, de.. Gioue:
Maeſtro di Cappella del Do-
mo di Padoua
ALL' ILLVSTRSSIMI
& Ecceilentiſſimi
SIG. PROCVRATORI
Di Chieſa di S. Marco.

In VENETIA, Preſſo Franceſco Miloco.
Con Lic. de Sup.   MDCXLIV.

CLAVDIO
MONTEVERDI

IX·V·MDLXVII   XXIX·XI·MDCXLIII

Monteverdi died in November 1643. He was given a lavish funeral, published (LEFT) with a titlepage filled with an interesting display of musical instruments. His grave is in S. Maria Gloriosa dei Frari, in the Chapel of the Milanesi, on the left-hand side. The inscription and bust are relatively recent.

After his death Monteverdi went out of fashion. The whole taste, style and way of looking at life underwent the most astonishing change. Venetian life in the 17th century was full of gravity: Monteverdi himself wrote gravely beautiful music. A century later paintings looked entirely different; love was entirely different; and music sounded entirely different.

Mozart and Beethoven never heard a note of Monteverdi and probably never even saw one of his publications. The resuscitation came gradually, towards the end of the 19th century. They discovered *L'incoronazione di Poppea* and Vincent d'Indy performed it in Paris.

They began to reprint Monteverdi. In the 1930s the famous French musician and teacher Nadia Boulanger made a set of records of madrigals, exquisitely sung, bringing Monteverdi into thousands of remote homes. The Universal Edition of Vienna, the great pioneer publishing house for modern music, took on the long task of issuing the complete works of Monteverdi, edited lovingly by Gian Francesco Malipiero, the Patrician Venetian composer who completed his task during the Second World War.

*   *   *

Unfortunately the performance of Monteverdi's music is not like, say, a Mozart symphony. When an orchestra plays a Mozart symphony the parts are distributed and the musicians play, loudly or softly, as Mozart wished, and phrase music with legato slurs and staccati according to the score. Many of Monteverdi's works have come down to us in what might be described as a shorthand form. To take one case in point which will serve for many others, we may consider the problem of *L'incoronazione di Poppea*. The opera was never printed in the 17th century, but two manuscripts have survived: one, previously thought to be Monteverdi's autograph, in the Marciana library in Venice; and a second one, in a copyist's hand in the library of the Conservatorio San Pietro a Majella in Naples. Recently, scholars have discovered that the handwriting of the Venetian copy is partly that of Monteverdi's star pupil, Piero Francesco Cavalli, who re-composed all the instrumental *sinfonie*. (The magnificent beginning of the opera is not by Monteverdi at all but is a composition of Cavalli's.) When Malipiero published his edition of *L'incoronazione di Poppea* in the Gesamtausgabe, he was under the impression that those autograph sections of the Venetian manuscript were by Monteverdi, and so every subsequent edition of the opera has incorporated all the Cavalli instrumental part music instead of the original music Monteverdi composed, which is preserved in the Neapolitan copy.

But our troubles have scarely begun; for neither copy of the opera specifies any instruments whatsoever. The instrumental pieces are written out in four or five parts with different clefs, but they do not say which instruments should play the individual lines. Moreover, although the vocal parts are complete, only the bass line, or, as it is called, basso continuo, has been included; and there is no indication of how many instruments should play in this basso continuo or when they should play. In other words, all that we have is a sort of musical skeleton, rather as if Beethoven's Fifth Symphony had come down to us only in the first

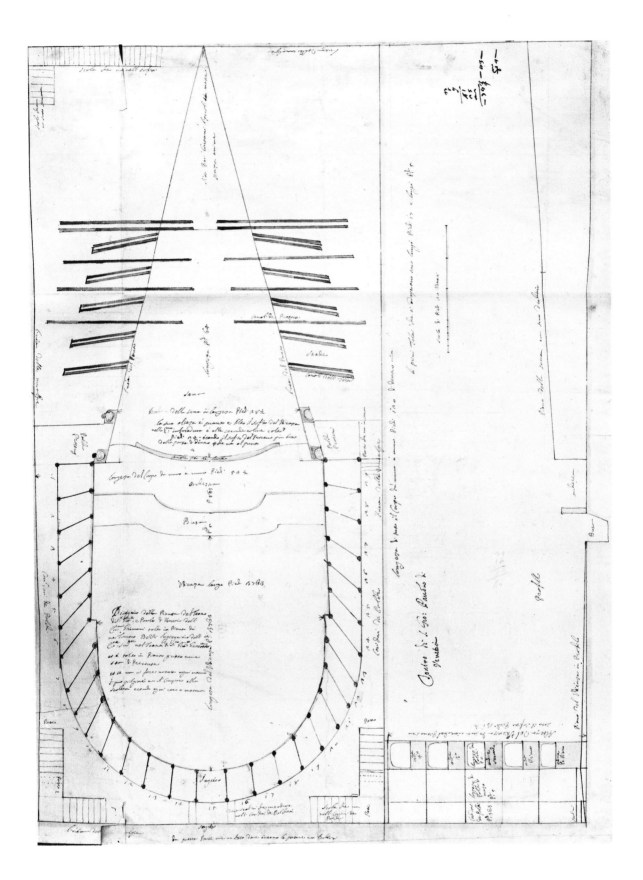

The Prologue to Poppea *in the Venetian manuscript is now known to be not by Monteverdi at all, but by his pupil and follower Francesco Cavalli. These instrumental interludes are probably in Cavalli's own hand.*

violin and bass parts. It is therefore quite impossible ever again to determine what Venetian audiences heard when they went to see *L'incoronazione di Poppea*; any attempt to present the work nowadays is of necessity a reconstruction. That is why there are at least ten versions of *L'incoronazione di Poppea* in circulation today. Some of these are opulently scored and sound barbarically magnificent: the version by Walter Goehr includes an enormous orchestra and no less than nine trombones, while other versions are content with two recorders, a couple of trumpets, strings, harpsichord and a flute. Even then our difficulties are not at an end, because Monteverdi's scores contain no dynamic marks and no phrasing marks, so that in a sense almost every piece of his has to be 'edited' before it can be performed. The success or failure of a modern Monteverdi performance therefore rests at least fifty per cent with the abilities of his modern editor; some of his editors have done him justice, and some have obviously not. It is well to remember that every gramophone record of Monteverdi represents at best an attempt to reconstruct what the scores must have sounded like. Of the works in question the best or easiest to produce are of course the madrigals, where it was not expected that instruments would necessarily double the voices. But even in the madrigals there are no dynamic marks to speak of and usually no tempo indications or any other mechanical aid to assist us in realizing their performance. It is, nevertheless, a tribute to the force and beauty of Monteverdi's music, that despite these almost superhuman difficulties, the sterling quality of his genius shines forth as brightly as it ever has in the last four hundred years.

*   *   *

Heinrich Schütz, the greatest German composer of his time, had first come to
Venice in 1600. From a contemporary biography we learn that he said that he had
noticed in himself a strong inclination towards the profession of noble music; and
since the world-famous composer, Giovanni Gabrieli, was still living in Venice
he, Herr Schütz, would be very pleased of an opportunity to go there and to
continue his studies there.[16] Schütz was Giovanni Gabrieli's star pupil, and the
great compositional link between Italy and Germany. His first published work
was in Venice, nineteen Italian madrigals, in 1611, when the composer was
twenty-six. How proud he must have been to see his name coming from a press

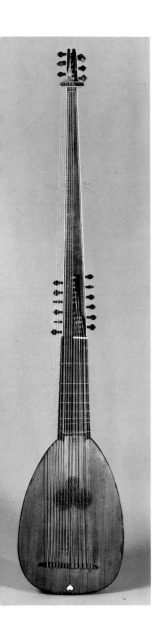

The lute family was the most numerous of the stringed instruments. Its largest member was the chitarrone, *often used to accompany singing.*

which had made Venetian music world-famous: *Il Primo Libro de Madrigali di Henrico Sagittario Allemanno In Venetia MDCXI Appresso Angelo Gardano & Fratelli.* The twelfth and last of these extremely sophisticated madrigals seems to be based on a text written by Schütz himself, and with the name of his German patron, Landgrave 'Maurizio' of Hesse cleverly woven into the proceedings. It is all music of a young man, the texts shining with youth, Spring and love – love's joys and love's sorrows, ladies' tears which are like marble.

In 1628 he came back to Venice, arriving on 11 August. It had taken him ten weeks to make the journey from Saxony because 'of the closed borders, not only in Germany but also in Venetian territory.'[17] He had come to buy 'much newer more beautiful music, since music which would be useful for the princely table, comedies, ballets and so on is infinitely better and more of it, as at the time I was first here . . .'[18] Nine months later he not only sent off music, but also instruments, and he recommended the 'best descant violinist', Francesco Castelli, for the Electorate service.[19]

His experiences of the second trip to Venice are summed up in the foreword to Sinfoniae Sacrae I, dedicated to the very musical Crown Prince, the 16-year-old Johann Georg II of Saxony: 'I was with my old friends in Venice, but found the style much changed. One tries to flatter the ear now, and I have tried to accustom my music to the new way . . .'[20]

He was particularly taken with old Monteverdi's style. 'The ingenious Herr Claudio Monteverdi' was, for the forty-three-year-old Schütz, the same venerated master as had been Giovanni Gabrieli during his first stay in Venice. Schütz took for his 'Es steht Gott auff' two themes of Monteverdi's madrigals 'Armato il cor' and 'Zefiro torna', but tells in the foreword that he has no intention to 'decorate my works with other birds' feathers.'[21]

We are not sure if Schütz, who was himself a celebrity in Venice, knew Monteverdi well, but his description of him as 'the most loveable human being and greatest artist in his metier' suggests that they had at least met.

*   *   *

Music continued to flourish in Venice even after Monteverdi's death. Opera in particular was greatly in demand. Venice possessed no less than six public opera houses, which were open throughout the Carnival, from Ascension Day to 15 June and during September and November. The price of a seat was only two lire and this new form of entertainment was very popular.

The opera composer wrote for an immediate audience. Few scores were printed – Monteverdi's *Orfeo* was a great exception – and performers worked mainly from copied manuscripts without mention of instruments. Instrumental accompaniment varied according to the nature and progress of the plot: violins for the lament, bassoons and trombones for the nether-world. The orchestra was not supposed to play while someone was singing, although passages in which sleep, magic, night or the underworld were depicted were regarded as exceptions. Recitatives were probably accompanied on a separate harpsichord played by the director.

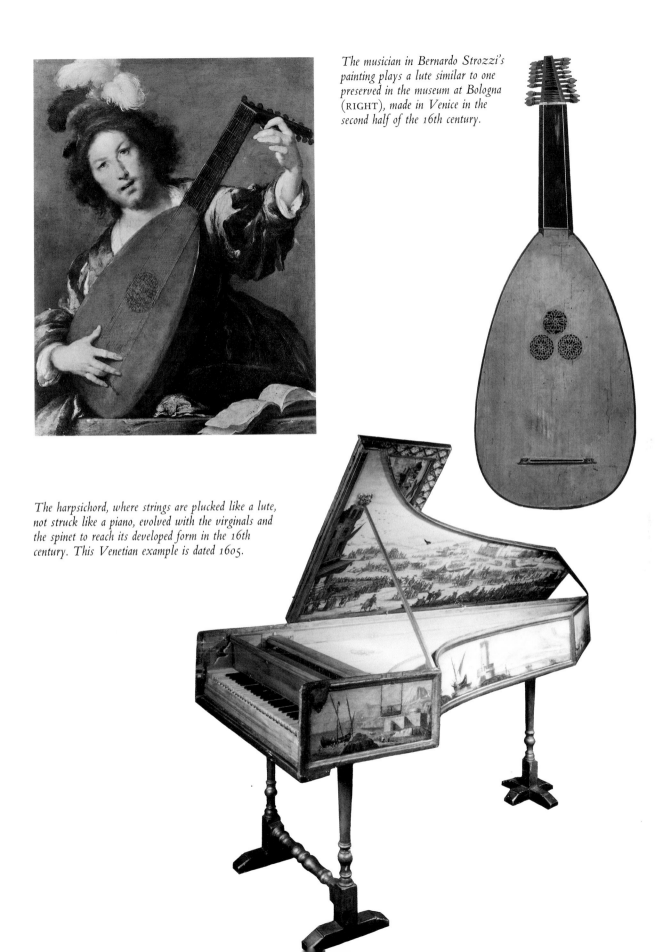

The musician in Bernardo Strozzi's painting plays a lute similar to one preserved in the museum at Bologna (RIGHT), made in Venice in the second half of the 16th century.

The harpsichord, where strings are plucked like a lute, not struck like a piano, evolved with the virginals and the spinet to reach its developed form in the 16th century. This Venetian example is dated 1605.

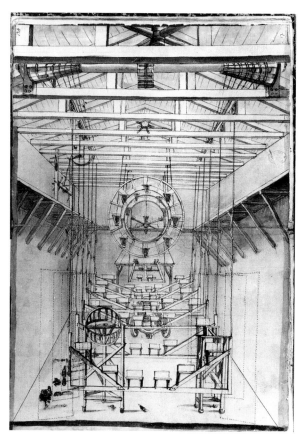

In 1676 Germanico sul Reno *by
Giovanni Legrenzi* (ABOVE) *was
produced at the Teatro San Salvatore,
Venice. These two drawings* (LEFT)
*show the machinery for one of the sets,
first without its painted scenery and then
with it. By means of a winch in the roof
the circular wooden frame could be lowered
onto the stage with the singers seated in it.
Other frames carry more characters at the
sides and there are two independent
structures left and right for special effects
(one man is flung out of a sphere onto the
ground).*

*Similarly amazing sets were made for
Cavalli's* Impermestro (RIGHT) *when it
was produced in Florence in 1658; one
simulated a whole town on fire, another the
hall of a magnificent palace.*

Proserpina Rapita ('The Rape of Proserpina') was another of Monteverdi's operas, composed for a wedding in the Palazzo Mocenigo in 1630. The words, by Giulio Strozzi, were published; the music, tantalizingly, was not, and is lost.

The average Venetian orchestra of the 17th century consisted of two violins, alto and tenor violins, violone, two theorbos and two or three harpsichords. By the final decades of the century ensemble instruments were being used in arias, in alternation with voices. Offstage instruments were also used for effect.

Ballets were shown between acts. In *Pompeo Magno* by Cavalli (1666) there were even dances for horses, madmen and phantoms.

Perhaps the most significant development, however, was in the use of arias. Monteverdi made extensive use of expressive recitative monologues and dialogues, adding only the occasional aria, usually for a minor character. His pupil Cavalli at first followed Monteverdi's style, but in the later part of his career made much greater use of arias, giving them an ever more prominent part in the opera and reducing the quantity of recitative considerably.

Cavalli's musical career began in 1617, at the age of fifteen, as a singer in Monteverdi's choir at San Marco. He wrote his first opera, *Le nozze di Teti e di Peleo* in 1639 and the following year became second Organist at San Marco. His long association with San Marco reached a peak in 1668 with his appointment to the post of *maestro di cappella*, which position he retained until his death in 1676 at the venerable age of seventy-four. He was the last of the *maestri di cappella* of San Marco to achieve fame as a great composer, and it is significant that it is for his secular works, his operas, that he is remembered; the age in which the Church was the main inspiration for music was drawing to a close.

No fewer than forty-two operas are attributed to Cavalli, the greater part of which were performed at the San Cassiano. He wrote in both comic and serious vein, and his work was immensely popular. The first real departure from Monteverdi's style occurred in 1650 when Cavalli discovered a new librettist, Nicolo Minato. Minato wrote texts which clearly demanded arias in some parts, and recitative in others. From then onwards Cavalli began to give a much greater prominence to arias. Opera, formerly a drama set to music, had taken its first steps towards becoming dramatic music. Venice could justly claim to be the mother of modern opera.[22]

Venice is also able to boast a great female composer, Barbara Strozzi.

Barbara was the apparently illegitimate daughter of Giulio Strozzi who had been one of Monteverdi's patrons and friends. He wrote the libretti for two lost operas by Monteverdi, including the first comic opera in the history of music, *La Licori Finta Pazza*.

Barbara, born in 1619, grew up using her presumed father's name and became the most celebrated female composer of her age (or indeed of any age – there are remarkably few women composers in the history of music). She studied with Francesco Cavalli and wrote music which was as attractive as any being published in mid-17th century. Barbara was also a beautiful woman, a celebrated hostess, and a member of one of Venice's academies, L'accademia degli Unisoni, called into being for her by her father.

The academies, which flourished all over Italy, discussed art, music, philosophy and love (in theoretical terms). Barbara was the hostess when the members discussed whether tears or song were the more potent weapon. One is sure that Barbara chose song.[23]

III   The Eighteenth Century

*T*he conquests of Francesco Morosini did not last long. In 1714 the Sultan once again declared war, and though Venice acquitted herself well – particularly at Corfu, where she defeated a vastly superior Turkish besieging force, inflicting heavy casualties – she once again emerged badly from the peace negotiations. By the Treaty of Passarowitz (1718) her imperial frontiers, such as they were, were drawn for the last time. Of her erstwhile Greek possessions, she retained only the Ionian Islands; for the rest, it was as if Morosini had never lived.

The 18th century was, therefore, an inglorious one for Venice, and not simply because it saw the end of the thousand-year Republic. The fact is that, by the time it was a quarter through its course, a people who had once been famous as the most skilful seamen and most courageous merchant adventurers that the world had ever seen were better known for their prowess as cheapskates and intriguers, gamblers and pimps. Nevertheless, there were compensations; and the greatest of these was the fact that for eighty years – thanks to wise government and successful diplomacy – Venice was at peace. Thus, with no wars to pay for, the economy flourished.

And so, once again, did the arts. Painting rose up once again from its 17th-century nadir: the city was celebrated as never before by the brilliance of the vedutisti, led by Canaletto and Francesco Guardi, while the old Venetian fascination with colour and light reached its apogee in the genius of Gian Battista Tiepolo. A city of some 160,000 people could boast no fewer than seven full-time opera houses, to say nothing of the theatres, in which the old commedia dell' arte was gradually giving place to the sophisticated domestic comedies of Venice's best-loved writer, Carlo Goldoni. By now, too, Venice had developed yet another art: that of elegant living. She had transformed herself into the pleasure capital of Europe, the place where Carnival continued for three months a year, the Las Vegas of her time; but it was a Las Vegas with a difference, saved by her people's natural good taste. Her values may not have been our values, her morals may have left a good deal to be desired; the fact remains that throughout the century hundreds – perhaps thousands – of the most cultivated and civilized men and women of Europe poured into the city every year. They cannot all have been wrong.

For this was, par excellence, the age of the Grand Tour. It was a European phenomenon, with the Alpine passes overrun every summer with the scions of all the great families of France and Germany, Austria and Scandinavia – but above all, perhaps, of England, whence a seemingly endless succession of young milords, accompanied by their tutors and valets, poured down annually into Italy. For most of them the ultimate goal was Rome – where, in the course of a Gibbonian autumn spent among the monuments of imperial decline, they would acquire a number of occasionally authentic pieces of classical sculpture and portraits of themselves by Raphael Mengs or Pompeo Batoni; but most of them made a point of keeping the Carnival in Venice, where they almost certainly left a fair proportion of their inheritance and what was left of their virginity – returning with the obligatory Canaletto and a mild dose of the clap.

At least where the Canaletto was concerned, they would have been obliged to seek the assistance of the English Consul, Joseph Smith. This extraordinary man had settled in Venice in 1700 at the age of eighteen, and lived there for the next seventy years. In 1740 he had moved into the palace now known as the Palazzo Mangilli-Valmarana, on the corner of the Grand Canal and the Rio dei Santi Apostoli, which had been designed for him by Antonio Visentini (better known as Canaletto's engraver) and which soon became the city's most astonishing private treasure-house, filled to overflowing with his ever-increasing collections of paintings and sculptures, coins and medals, drawings and cameos, books and prints. Apart from these there were always additional works by his personal protégés – the brothers Marco and Sebastiano Ricci, Francesco Zuccarelli, the pastel portraitist Rosalba Carriera and, above all, Canaletto himself – for whom he acted as chief agent and go-between with their patrons among the English nobility. It was thanks to him that nearly all Canaletto's best work is in England; no wonder that he was the dedicatee of the master's only published collection of engravings. But Britain's debt to Smith goes far beyond this: in 1762 he sold his collections en masse to George III for £20,000 – 'the most spectacular acquisition by an English royal collector', writes Sir Oliver Millar, 'since Charles I's agent had brought off his coup in Mantua in the 1620s'. Three years later the King followed this tremendous purchase with another: that of Smith's entire library, bought for a further £10,000, which forms the nucleus of the British Library today. And even this did not mark the end of the Consul's collecting career; he immediately began amassing new treasures, and after his death in 1770 the sale of his new library alone took thirteen days.

At that time Napoleon Buonaparte was a one-year-old baby in Corsica; but only twenty-six years later he was given command of a French army with orders to drive the Austrians out of Italy. With the capture of Milan two months later, he had virtually all Lombardy in his hands. Now only the neutral territory of Venice lay between him and the imperial frontier. Suddenly the Venetians found themselves in serious danger. They knew they had no chance against this apparently invincible young general: their one hope would have been to accept his offer of alliance. Unaccountably, however, they refused; and from that moment their death warrant was sealed.

The story of Venice's downfall does her little credit. Her courage, her resolution, her diplomatic skills all deserted her. By turns she allowed herself to be bullied, bluffed and browbeaten. On Friday 12 May 1797 the Great Council met for the last time, and for the most fateful decision in its history – to decide whether to accept Napoleon's ultimatum, which demanded the abolition of the Republic and the occupation of their city by French troops. The Council was still in session when firing was heard outside. Though the fusillade proved in fact to be nothing more than a farewell salute by departing Dalmatian troops, it was enough to cause the meeting to break up in disorder. Most of the members fled; but Doge Lodovico Manin simply withdrew to his private apartments, where he slowly removed the ducal corno from his head and handed it to his valet with the words which, more than any others, seem to symbolize the fall of Venice: 'Tolè, questa no la dopero più': 'Take it, I shall not be needing it again.'

25, 26, 27   *Venice was expected to put on a magnificent show, and she never disappointed. In 1782 the Grand Duke of Russia, the future Tsar Paul I, arrived in Venice. He and his wife were travelling incognito under the charming but not very convincing names of the Count and Countess of the North. Of course, their true identity was known to everyone and huge festivities were held in their honour. One grand reception was given at the Teatro S. Benedetto, recorded in a painting by Antonio Baratti* (LEFT). *A flight of steps has been placed in front of the stage but otherwise the theatre, with its four tiers of boxes and proscenium arch, is depicted as it was. Even the orchestra pit has its musicians. Giandomenico Tiepolo's* Carnival Scene (ABOVE) *and Longhi's* Dance *convey the same atmosphere of sophisticated, slightly stage-managed gaiety.*

28, 29   *Antonio Vivaldi was the great master
of the violin, not only playing it superbly
himself but also teaching it and writing music
that extended its technical possibilities and gave
soloists almost infinite opportunities for
expression and display. His great work*
L'Estro Armonico *is a complete
demonstration of everything the violin could do.
J.S. Bach did not scruple to learn from it,
copying many of Vivaldi's concertos and
arranging them for his own purposes.*

When a group of girls from one of the
ospedali, *trained by Vivaldi or a teacher of
comparable status, played for fashionable 18th-
century Venice, the scene must have looked very
much as Longhi portrays it* (RIGHT). *The
Rococo spirit expressed itself in every aspect of
life and culture — in painting, in decoration, in
the women's dresses and in Vivaldi's music.
Played in a modern concert hall, this totality is
inevitably lost.*

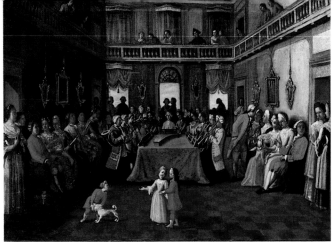

30   Concerts could take place in the halls of
noblemen's homes (LEFT) which typically for
Venice would have three large doors opening onto
balconies overlooking the canal. Here the various
instruments are shown with some care, the
harpsichordist directing the ensemble from the
middle.

31, 32, 33, 34,   Opera was of two kinds, opera
seria, with recitatives and opera buffa, with
spoken dialogue. Opera seria had the greater
prestige. Its characters were kings and princes and
its stories drawn from the classics, history or
poetry. A Venetian theatrical scene (CENTRE
LEFT) shows such a performance, with the
audience — many paying only scant attention.
    Two scenes of informal music-making.
ABOVE harpsichord music on a balcony, portrayed
on an 18th-century Venetian plate. LEFT a concert
at home, listened to by the family dog. RIGHT the
view that Goldoni would have seen through his
window. The house where he was born — now the
Palazzo Centani — was bought by the state in
1914 and is preserved as a museum of the Venetian
theatre.

After the ravages of the 17th century Venice spent the greater part of the 18th century at peace. One final show of force with the Turks in 1714 resulted in the loss of the greater part of the Republic's remaining territory in the Aegean, and thereafter the Doge and Senate took great care to avoid becoming involved in any conflicts.

Venetians could not fail to see that the Republic's glory had faded. Dissatisfaction with the constitution and with the extravagance and corruption of the ruling powers grew. The city itself was falling into decay. Gibbon's description of the city was typical of most visitors' reaction to it: 'old and in general ill-built houses, ruined pictures and stinking ditches . . . a fine bridge [the Rialto] spoilt by two rows of houses upon it, and a large square decorated with the worst architecture I ever saw.'[1]

In trade Venice found herself at a disadvantage as rapid advances in shipbuilding techniques elsewhere in Europe rendered the oared galley ship, which had formerly served the Venetians so well, obsolete. It became necessary for Venice to build a new line of ships, and to alter their trading attitudes. In 1736 the Republic finally faced up to the fact that it could no longer control the Aegean, and abandoned its old protectionist policies. With greater freedom of trade, the Venetians began taking up transit trade in articles such as wine, dried fruit and sulphur from the Adriatic.

In 1705 Addison wrote about Venetian trade and shipping:

Their trade is far from being in a flourishing condition; and there are high duties laid on merchandise. Their nobles think it beneath them to engage in traffic: their merchants who are grown rich, buy the honour of nobility, and generally give over trade: Their manufactures are silk, cloth, and glass, which were formerly the best in Europe, but are now excelled by those of other countries: They are tenacious of their old laws and customs, while a trading nation should be always making new changes as different emergencies arise.

. . . The arsenal of Venice is an island of about three miles in compass, which contains all their stores and provisions for war that are not actually employed. There are docks for their men of war and galleys, as well as workhouses for all preparations both by sea and land. The building in which the arms are deposited, makes a great shew, and about 100 years ago was an extraordinary place, but great part of its furniture is now grown useless. There seemed to be near as many suits of armour as there are guns, many of the swords are old fashioned and unwieldy, and the fire arms fitted with locks that are not to be compared with those that are now in use. The Venetians pretend, they could in case of necessity fit out 30 men of war, 100 galleys and 10 galeasses: but it is not easy to conceive how they could man half the number.[2]

35 OPPOSITE *The interior of San Marco, by Canaletto; scene of the first performances of so many musical masterpieces.*

If Venice was in decline during the 18th century, very few
visitors noticed it. True, she had lost her Mediterranean
empire and her monopoly of trade with the Far East. She
was no longer a great power. But she was still a prosperous
and flourishing city. Guardi's painting of the Molo (LEFT)
shows a quayside crowded with ships, even though they are
now the great ocean-going vessels that had stripped her of her
naval supremacy. And the Rialto (BELOW), the very centre
of Venice, still teemed with merchants from all over the
world. Spanning the Grand Canal and lined with shops, it
was the only link between the two halves of Venice.

By the end of the century Venice had developed a major local shipping trade, but she was best known throughout the 18th century as a centre for revelry and high living.

Her earlier reputation for courtesans had grown to the extent that Venice was described as the 'brothel of Europe'. Lady Mary Wortley Montague, writing to the Countess of Pomfret in 1739 stated that 'it is so much the fashion for everybody to live their own way, that nothing is more ridiculous than censuring the actions of another'.[3]

One convincing theory explains this attitude by the hereditary practices of the Venetian nobility:

It has been calculated that, as early as the sixteenth century, 51 per cent of noble Venetians remained unmarried; in the seventeenth century this figure rose to 60 per cent; in the eighteenth to 66 per cent. The underlying philosophy is clear. The family must continue; and it must continue rich. One son – often the youngest – was therefore required to marry, and to beget enough legitimate heirs to ensure the first of these requirements; the other sons would remain single – or at least childless – thus by preventing the dispersal of wealth, fulfilling the second. This enforced bachelorhood may well have accounted for the number of professional courtesans in Venice – as opposed to the regiments of whores that are part and parcel of any flourishing sea-port. It certainly explains the quantity of 'orphanages'.[4]

Addison commented on a different aspect of the same practice:

The nobility spreads equally through all the brothers, and they generally thrust the females of their families into convents, the better to preserve their estates. Hence the Venetian Nuns are famous for the liberties they allow themselves. They have operas within their own walls, and if they are not much misrepresented, often go out of their bounds to meet their admirers.[5]

The freedom from censure, noted by Lady Mary, extended to other pleasures too. Addison again:

The great diversions at Venice during the carnival, as well as on other extraordinary occasions, is masking; for though the Venetians are naturally grave, they love to give into the follies and entertainments of such seasons when dignified in a false personage; and indeed they are under a necessity of finding out such diversions as may agree with their situation, and make them some amends for the loss of these pleasures which may be met with upon the continent. These disguises occasion abundance of love adventures, and there is something more intriguing in the amours of Venice than in those of other countries. Operas are another great entertainment at this season; the music is good.[6]

The era of the Grand Tour was in full swing, and young travellers from all parts of Europe flocked to Venice, ostensibly to finish their education by a study of its art and architecture, but usually receiving a rather more worldly education. Night and day, Venice provided entertainment and spectacle to feed the appetites of its visitors. One of them, J.B.S. Morritt, wrote:

The hours of their amusements are insufferable, and we find it a great bore to go to the opera, which does not begin till eleven and lasts till three or four; and what do you think must be the spirit of the public balls which are given after the opera sometimes?[7]

Venetian convents were not quite what one would expect today. They were rich, almost aristocratic establishments where girls received a better education than if they remained with their parents. Rules were relaxed. This lively picture by Guardi shows pupils receiving visitors on the other side of a grille. Music was an important part of their curriculum.

Two young sisters, Elizabeth and Eugenia Wynne, visiting Venice in 1790, made the following entries in their diaries for 15 February:

Elizabeth: 'Went to the opera at St Benetto and run about the boxes always masked in the Italian fashion. They made a great furore for Mrs Banti they throwed verses in her praise, Peacocks, Pols, Pigeons and golden raise was thrown to.'

Eugenia: 'Dressed very soon [as] a Shepherdess. Stoped very long for our Cavalier Servants which are the sons of the Embassador of france. Walked in the place of St. Marc . . . Papa was dressed in weomen's clothes. . . . There was a great quantity of people . . . We see a little girl with two faces and behind she is as well formed as any child can be she has got to legs a coming out from her breast for the rest she is very well shaped . . . There is a man that comes down from the top of the Campanil on St Marc on a rope and gieves a nosguay to the Doge and then they make some very good fireworks.'[8]

Even the personalities of the day were extravagant and colourful. Canaletto, the greatest of Venice's artists, drunk with the success of his work, would trifle with his customers, raising or decreasing his prices according to his mood, and delivering the finished work when and as he pleased. Vivaldi, one of the most popular 18th-century composers, was a priest who despite being too ill to be able to conduct mass, was suspected of having several mistresses.

The Carnival drew visitors from all over Europe. The Venetian government — strict, even ruthless, in everything to do with political power — seems to have encouraged the pursuit of pleasure as a way of defusing possible discontent. At Carnival time everyone wore a mask. Anonymity gave freedom. The sexes and the social classes could mix outside the constraints of ordinary conventions. Moralists called it licentious, and indeed it was. But it was popular, and no subject is more widely celebrated in painting. RIGHT the Ridotto, or public assembly, by Guardi. BELOW RIGHT a similar genre scene showing card games in progress. BELOW LEFT one of Giandomenico Tiepolo's paintings of Venetian life. A band plays in the open air while a man and woman apparently keep a secret assignation. The oboist in the centre seems to be beating time.

*Animal shows (ABOVE) and
puppets (BELOW) both required
musical accompaniment of a
fairly basic kind. RIGHT an
open-air stage at the foot of the
Campanile.*

*OPPOSITE café life in the
Piazza San Marco, under the
arcades of the Procuratie Nuove,
has not changed much in 250
years. The way the man in the
cloak holds the saucer of his
coffee-cup is particularly elegant.*

Another tourist, John Moore, described the scene in the Piazza San Marco:

In the evening there generally is on St. Mark's place, such a mixed multitude of Jews,
Turks, and Christians; lawyers, knaves, and pick-pockets; mountebanks, old women
and physicians; women of quality with masks; strumpets barefaced; and, in short, such a
jumble of senators, citizens, gondoliers and people of every character and condition, that
your ideas are broke, bruised and dislocated in the crowd, in such a manner that you can
think, or reflect on nothing, yet this being a state of mind which many people are fond of,
the place never fails to be well attended and in fine weather numbers pass a great part of
the night there. When the piazza is illuminated and the shops in the adjacent streets are
lighted up, the whole has a brilliant effect; and as it is the custom for the ladies, as well as
the gentlemen to frequent the casinos and the coffee houses around, the place of St. Mark
answers all the purposes of either Vauxhall or Ranelagh.[9]

The regatta was a race between gondoliers starting at the far end of the Molo near the Giardini Pubblici, going all the way up the Grand Canal, turning and coming back as far as the Ca' Foscari (ABOVE), *where the race finished. This is one of the Venetian traditions that is still kept up.*

Such was the Venetian love of pomp and revelry that even the threat of an imminent French invasion could not stop them from celebrating the Ascension Day feast in usual style as shown by this extract from J.B.S. Morritt's description of his Grand Tour:

At Venice we are quiet, but people are packing up their tatters in great haste from most of the other parts of Italy, as they fear, when the French have seized the mouth of the boot, that they may not be able to get out at the toes. Besides the neutrality of Venice (which seems not to be treated with any great respect) we console ourselves that we have a nice back door to creep out at even though Verona is seized, for we can always get into a Trieste boat, and a very few hours sets the Adriatic between us. In the meantime we are going to-day to see the Doge marry that fair lady. The ceremony generally takes place at the Ascension, but his wife was not in the humour, and seemed to pout and fret so much that he dares not approach her. To-day she is in a more winning mood, though not very serene . . . We here [Piazza San Marco] found the Doge and Senators filing two by two on board the Bucentaur, the large state galley used for this purpose. This galley is covered with a red velvet canopy, and every part of it very fine, with a prodigious quantity of carving and gilding. When they were all on board it was rowed and towed slowly out to the Lido . . . It was attended by thousands of gondolas and other barges, which made the scene very gay and pretty, especially as several of the Venetian ladies were in them, and were no bad change after the ugly faces we have been used to at Naples and Rome.

At a church, which is on one of the islands about two miles off, the Doge and his train descended after the ceremony of dropping a ring into the Adriatic, and heard High Mass, during which we amused ourselves with walking about and looking at people's pretty faces on the island.[10]

The final sentence shows how far the ceremony had ceased to be a religious festival for many of the spectators. Indeed the Carnival and the saints' days

celebrations, which had originated as religious festivals, were now major tourist attractions. Pope Gregory XIII, despairing of the Venetians' morals, said 'I am Pope everywhere except in Venice.'

The centre of musical activity in Venice had also moved away from San Marco, to the Orphanages.

There were four orphanages for girls in Venice; the Pietà, the Incurabili, the Mendicanti and the Ospedaletto. They had been opened during the Crusades as hostels (*ospidali*) for pilgrims, but later became orphanages for foundling girls. In these institutions the Platonic theory of education was followed, and music was included in the curriculum. By the 18th century the standard was recognized to be so high that the nobility sought places for their daughters as paying students.

The Pietà was the best known of the four (and the employer of Vivaldi, who was the violin master there during the first half of the century). Its music staff consisted of a director for the choir, an organist, and teachers for violin, viola, oboe, psaltery, transverse flute, cello, clarinets, horn and timpani. Students entering the conservatories attached to the orphanages would be taught first by senior girls, then by the masters. The students played and sang for chapel service and also gave concerts when the theatres were not in season.

The Mendicanti, situated near the church of SS. Giovanni e Paolo, used *piffari* instruments, which were not employed in the theatre orchestras or the Pietà orchestra. It also taught keyboard instruments and its choir performed oratorios. Most of the musical staff at the Mendicanti were ranking musicians at San Marco. Galuppi was *Maestro di Coro* there from 1740–51.

Of the Incurabili and Ospedaletto little is known, except that the Incurabili was at the height of its popularity in the middle of the 18th century.

* * *

The most splendid of all Venetian festivals was the Marriage of Venice to the Adriatic. Reputedly going back to the 12th century, it took place annually on Ascension Day. The Doge, in the great barge known as the Bucintoro, was rowed to the mouth of the Lido where he threw a ring into the sea. In Guardi's painting he is seen approaching the Lido and the old church of S. Niccolò.

The orphanages were the centres of Venetian musical life, as
interest shifted from the sacred to the secular. The Pietà, the
Incurabili, the Mendicanti and the Ospedaletto all had orchestras
and choirs and employed the best musicians as teachers. Vivaldi
taught the violin at the Pietà. The music room of the Ospedaletto
(OPPOSITE ABOVE) preserves its singing galleries and grilles;
the painting at the end is by the studio of Tiepolo and represents
classical exponents of music. LEFT The Singing Lesson by
Longhi. ABOVE a concert in the Philharmonic Hall, with the girls
in the balconies above, those in the front row playing violins.
RIGHT instruction in singing to one's own accompaniment.

Antonio Vivaldi, the most famous of all Venetian composers, was born in March 1678 and baptized in the church of S. Giovanni in Bragora (ABOVE RIGHT). His father was a violinist at San Marco (OPPOSITE, by Canaletto, who shows the choir singing in a gallery from an enormous book). Vivaldi was ordained a priest, but devoted himself full-time to music.

The greatest representative of 18th-century Venetian music was an enigma. To hundreds of Venetian foundling girls, he was music-master; to a Protestant cantor named Johann Sebastian Bach, he was a most honoured colleague; to his Italian colleagues he was almost a defrocked priest. His name was Antonio Vivaldi.

Vivaldi was born in Venice on a day when an earthquake shook the lagoon city, March 4, 1678. Of all the composers whom Venice has brought forth, none – not even the famous Gabrieli family or Domenico Cimarosa – has achieved the widespread acclaim now given the man whom his contemporaries called *il prete rosso*, 'the red priest'.

The red hair must have been inherited, for Antonio's father, Giovanni Battista – a baker's son who after starting life in his father's profession, abandoned it to become a musician – was referred to as 'Rossi' (red head) or 'Giovanni Battista Rossi' when he was engaged as a violinist at San Marco. One of several children, Antonio was – from the first – destined for the priesthood, despite the fact that he was a sickly child, suffering from '*strettezza di petto*' (literally, 'tightness of the chest') which is now thought to have been either asthma or angina pectoris. On September 18, 1693, Antonio took holy orders and was ordained on March 23, 1703. He trained for the priesthood with the Fathers of S. Giovanni in Oleo, but apparently, as a result of his weak condition, received a special dispensation to remain at home with his parents in the district of S. Martino. Even at this early stage, while training for the Church, he seems to have practised music, substituting as violinist for his father at San Marco. Apart from studying violin with his father, Antonio had as his principal master the well-known organist and composer of Venice, Giovanni Legrenzi, admired by Bach (who used a theme by Legrenzi as a fugal subject for an organ piece).

The first violin part of Vivaldi's Suonate da Camera, published in Venice in 1705.

Two years after his ordination, Vivaldi published his first music, Opus 1, twelve trio sonatas dedicated to a local nobleman, Count Annibale Gambara; it was issued by a well-known Venetian house, Sala. By this time, the composer was well-known to the connoisseurs of his native city, and he had also found a way to reconcile his calling with his vocation. (Not that it was considered wrong or even eccentric for a priest to be engaged in musical activity, but Vivaldi's case was special: as a result of his illness, he could hardly even stay on his feet long enough to say Mass – or so we are told.)

'Because of this *strettezza di petto*, I nearly always remain at home,' wrote Vivaldi to a patron, 'and my travels have always been most expensive because I have always had to undertake them with four or five persons in assistance.' This crippling affliction also forced him to give up saying Mass, 'since on three occasions I have had to leave the altar without completing it because of this ailment.'[11] This dual life, musician and priest, was to be his curious lot throughout life, and finally it was to get him into tremendous difficulties. No one doubted Vivaldi's religious fervour; indeed, in the privacy of his study, he signed his scores 'In Nomine Domini' and ended them with the same set of religious initials ('Praise be to the Blessed Virgin Mary . . .') as did Bach and Haydn. The famous Venetian poet and playwright, Carlo Goldoni, whose scintillating and witty libretti were to change the entire face of Italian spoken theatre as well as *opera buffa*, once went to call on Vivaldi:

I went to Abbé Vivaldi's house and found him surrounded by music and with his breviary in his hand. He rose, made the complete sign of the Cross, put down his breviary, and made me the usual compliments. [After a short opening conversation], the Abbe took up his breviary once more, made another sign of the Cross, and did not answer.

'Signor' I said, 'I don't wish to disturb you in your religious pursuits; I shall come another time'. [Vivaldi continued the conversation] however, walking about with his breviary, reciting his psalms and hymns . . .[12]

As luck would have it, Vivaldi was able to find a position that easily reconciled his priestly garb with the violin. In September 1703, he was engaged as *maestro di violino* at an extraordinary Venetian institution, the Conservatory of the Ospedale della Pietà.

This 'hospital', affectionately referred to by its Italian diminutive, *ospedaletto*, was something like the London Foundling Hospital of Handelian fame. Venice boasted four such hospitals, as we have seen; they were charitable institutions originally founded to receive orphaned (and largely illegitimate) girls – often dumped on the doorstep – give them an education at the city's expense, and then, if possible, see that they were married when they reached a suitable age. Gradually, the Pietà became, to all intents and purposes, the best music school in northern Italy. Its atmosphere seems to have been gay and frivolous as only a Venetian institution of this kind could be. A British traveller, writing in the early 1720s (when Vivaldi's fame was at its height), writes:

Those who would choose for a wife one that has not been acquainted with the world go to these places to look for them, and they generally take all the care they can, they shall be

Carlo Goldoni, whose brilliant comedies written both in polite Italian and in Venetian patois are still performed, knew Vivaldi well and has left an amusing description of a visit to him.

as little acquainted with the world afterwards . . . Every Sunday and holiday there is a performance of music in the chapels of these hospitals, vocal and instrumental, performed by the young women of the place, who are set in a gallery above and, though not professed, are hid from any distinct view of those below by a lattice of ironwork. The organ parts, as well as those of the other instruments are all performed by the young women. They have a eunuch for their master and he composes most of their music. Their performance is surprisingly good . . . and this is all the more amusing since their persons are concealed from view.[13]

Vivaldi lived in this district, the Campo S. Giuseppe, on the eastern edge of Venice.

A famous picture by Guardi conjures up better than any words this carefree and happy atmosphere. Although the young ladies were supposedly 'cloistered like nuns', manners in the Pietà seem to have been rather free and easy.

Jean-Jacques Rousseau, also a musician/composer, even managed to get himself smuggled into the girls' premises for supper and though he found them supremely ugly (one was 'horrible'), they were 'not without charm'.[14] Another writer, mentioning that many of these orphans had been forced to take the veil, says that 'even after having taken their vows they maintained worldly practices and dressed elegantly . . . their bosoms only half covered by narrow pleated bodices of silk . . . The stillness of the cloister was sometimes broken . . . by the merry shouts of the young aristocrats as they danced with the nuns, and would go so far as to stay out all night with their lovers.'[15]

Of all the orphanages in Venice, that of the Pietà had the highest reputation for music. A British traveller of the 1720s describes how the girls performed in a gallery 'hid from any distinct view of those below by a lattice of ironwork.' The present church of the Pietà (BELOW and OPPOSITE) was designed by Giorgio Massari and built between 1745 and 1760. It is notable for its oval plan and the latticed balcony which still encircles the interior.

BENEDICTUS MARCELLO
PATRITIUS VENETUS
Anno 1712 inter Academ Phÿarm cooptat obiit anno 1739.

Francesco Gasparini, a notable composer in his own right, was Vivaldi's predecessor as maestro di concerti *at the* Pietà. *This sketch is by the caricaturist Pier Leone Ghezzi.*

Benedetto Marcello, *a pupil of Gasparini, specialized in church music and took a poor view of Vivaldi and the modernists. He wrote a satirical pamphlet against them called* Il Teatro alla Moda. *His own best-known works (featured in this portrait) were fifty paraphrases of the Psalms.*

Vivaldi managed to secure this (rather modestly paid) position, which gave him sixty ducats per annum, because the musical director of the Pietà, the then celebrated composer, Francesco Gasparini from Lucca, told the institution's directors that they needed teachers for the violin and oboe. Vivaldi taught the violin, of course, and in August 1704, his salary was raised by forty ducats because his duties now included teaching the young ladies the viole all'inglese, a family of larger and smaller string instruments like the viola d'amore, with sympathetic vibrating strings located behind the fingerboard.

Meanwhile, Venice was host to an illustrious royal visitor: King Frederick IV of Denmark, who arrived on December 30, 1708 and attended a concert at the Pietà the same evening. To him Vivaldi dedicated his Opus 2 violin sonatas, which appeared the following year. By 1708–9, he was composing those concertos for various instruments which soon became famous throughout Europe: violin concertos for himself and concertos for other instruments – flute, oboe, violoncello, bassoon, even two horns – to be played by the talented young ladies half visible behind the lattice-work of the Pietà's church.

Vivaldi's lean and wiry concertos were often performed not only in the salon, but in church as well, for instance as a substitute for the Gradual or Offertory. Baroque Italy found nothing incongruous in Maestro Vivaldi's playing a virtuoso concerto for the violin with a dazzling cadenza during a church service; indeed, one such concerto is entitled 'Fatto per la Solennità della S. Lingua di S. Antonio in Padova ('written for the solemn festival of the sacred tongue of Saint Anthony in Padua').

His relations with the Pietà were, to say the least, tenuous. For, in February 1709 he was dismissed, or rather his position made redundant. Two and a half years later, however, in September 1711, he was re-elected and remained in the job until March 1716 against steadily increasing opposition. (Vivaldi's position was given out by a majority vote among the directors of the institution.) A few months later, in May 1716, the composer was given a new position at the *ospedaletto*, one entitled *maestro de'concerti* ('master of musick' would have been an 18th-century British equivalent); this position came Vivaldi's way because Gasparini had, one month earlier, obtained sick leave; and in the event he never returned. Gasparini's absence now enabled Vivaldi to compose church music for the Pietà. During the previous year, in June 1715, the directors had given Vivaldi a special fee of fifty ducats for 'an entire mass, a vespers, an oratorio, over 3 motets and other efforts'.

Vivaldi's fame soon began to spread far beyond his native land. As we have said, his first published works, Opus 1 and 2, came out in Venice, printed in the old-fashioned 'music type' in use there for centuries. But about 1711, the composer moved his publishing activities to a much greater centre for music printing, Amsterdam, where the up-to-date firm of Roger (later succeeded by La Cene) was selling engraved music all over Europe.

Vivaldi specially mentions Roger's new technique in their first collaboration; Opus 3. It was the single most influential music publication of its time — concertos for various combinations of strings dedicated to Ferdinand Grand Duke of Tuscany. The nervous, tight rhythm of the quick movements; the fastidious, thin texture of the melancholic slow movements (like the grey of Venice in winter); the brilliant string technique with those virtuoso figurations, broken chords and 'flashy' violin tricks; all these fascinating innovations spread Opus 3 like wildfire throughout northern Europe. By the 1720s Vivaldi's music was not only popular all over Europe, but in some countries, such as France, there was a real Vivaldi cult — just as today.

Bach transcribed no less than five of Vivaldi's Opus 3 for organ, and Vivaldi's concerto for four violins and orchestra from the same set became, in Bach's hands, an equally astonishing Concerto for four harpsichords and orchestra in A minor. (As matters would turn out, it was the renewed interest in Bach in the 19th century, that led first scholars and then performers to the magic world of Vivaldi, then totally forgotten except in history books and on archive shelves.)

Further works published in Amsterdam followed: Opus 4, c.1714; *La Stravaganza*, dedicated to Vettor Dolfin, Vivaldi's pupil from the Venetian aristocracy; six Concertos for strings; then between 1716 and 1717, six sonatas and over six concertos for five instruments. Opus 8 followed in 1725; *Il cimento del'armonia e dell'inventione* (the Struggle between Harmony and Invention), dedicated to Count Wenzeslaus von Morzin, an Austro-Bohemian nobleman for whose family Haydn was a Kapellmeister more than a quarter of a century later. Vivaldi became a kind of long-distance 'maestro in Italia, dell'Illustrissimo Conte' to Count Morzin. This Opus 8 includes 'The Four Seasons' which has become one of the most popular pieces of 18th-century music since its spectacular resuscitation in our times. It is the first great instance of programme music (in the

widest sense) in Vivaldi's oeuvre and created a profound impression throughout Europe.

In the four years between 1727 and 1731, Vivaldi's output was substantial; six flute concertos, which were not only very popular but created a whole new standard for the flute concerto as a form, were followed by twelve violin concertos.

Vivaldi's father was an opera composer (on a modest scale) and an operatic entrepreneur; so that it is natural that Vivaldi should have turned his attention to what was potentially a very lucrative side to his second profession. He began his operatic career in Vicenza with a work entitled *Ottone in Villa*, in May 1713. There followed a long series of operatic commissions in northern Italy; he ended up with over forty-five operas to his credit, though none has ever entered the permanent repertoire.

It was later during this period that Vivaldi became associated with a young contralto singer named Anna Giraud (or, as the Italians prefer, 'Girò'). She became his protégée, possibly when she was at the Pietà, for contemporary sources refer to her as 'Annina della Pietà'. Her sister, Paolina, soon became the composer's nurse. Since both girls had become part of the Vivaldi 'entourage' tongues were wagging and even the church became scandalized when it heard, and heard repeatedly, that both girls alternated for the Red Priest's favours other than musical. The clerical authorities tried to ban them from appearing in Ferrara in 1737–8. Even though Vivaldi's defence is curiously touching, is it believable that such an 'innocent' could write an opera of the power and intensity of *Orlando Furioso*?

Obviously we can never know the truth, but it just might be that Vivaldi's relationship to the sisters was what he professed it to be – completely platonic. On the other hand, he could have been enjoying two pretty mistresses. Whichever way, he was not always very discreet.

To continue with Vivaldi's career: although his Amsterdam publishers were now issuing his music at their expense, paying him a generous fee (which was a rarity in those days, composers generally engraved and published their music at their own expense), Vivaldi began to find that he could do better by selling his works individually and in manuscript copies. He was dissatisfied with the usual way of publication, he told a visiting British traveller, Edward Holdsworth, for he could command the fee of one guinea for every manuscript copy of the concerto.

Vivaldi had dedicated his Opus 9 to none other than the Emperor Charles VI whom he met in 1728, possibly in the Adriatic seaport of Trieste. Charles thought highly of the Venetian and was possibly his host in Vienna, perhaps in 1730.

Between 1729 and 1738, Vivaldi spent a good deal of his time abroad travelling to Germany with his father, residing in Ferrara with the Giraud sisters (and probably others in the entourage) and even returning to Amsterdam to play his violin concertos for the centenary of the Schouwburg Theatre. Although he was in Venice between 1733 and 1775, again as the principal composer of S. Angelo, his long association with the Pietà was officially terminated in 1738, possibly because he was abroad so much. As we can see, for someone who was so afflicted with illness that he was unable to finish Mass, he did a great deal of travelling. But his association with the Pietà was shortly to be restored.

In 1739, Vivaldi was now producing operas in Venice, but contemporaries tell us that he had gone out of fashion. The theatres and ridotti of Venice were now welcoming the very fashionable comedies of Goldoni. These brilliant and unstilted pieces known as 'Commedie dell'Arte' put the life-style of the average Venetian's drawing room on the stage for the first time. They had their own musical accompaniments which were never outstanding in any way, but which hardly mattered. The audiences loved them.

In December 1739, shortly before Vivaldi left Venice for the last time, Prince Frederick Christian, King of Poland and Elector of Saxony, came to Venice. There was an elaborate concert at the Pietà; all the surrounding canals were illuminated; Vivaldi presented a series of new works, for which he received fifteen ducats and thirteen lire. (The King took the works back to Dresden and they are among the most valuable Vivaldiana that we have today, known in musical circles as the 'Dresden' Concertos.)

An engraved portrait of Vivaldi, 1724, and (RIGHT) *a French watercolour, undated but of the 18th century, showing a 'new concert hall in Venice'.*

LUMEN A LUMINE
LUMINIBUS ADRIAE.
D.

Veduta del magnifico Apparato e Illuminazione del Teatro in S. Samuele, tutto ornato di Specchi a disegno, con quadrature, bassi rilevi bracciali e Scena trasparente di Cristalli il tutto ideato, eseguito, e dedicato alla NOBILTA VENETA da Antonio Codognato Veneziano nell' Anno MDCCLIII.

Apparently Vivaldi had his eye on Austria. As his popularity had waned in his native land, his Amsterdam publishers were no longer anxious to publish his new concertos and sonatas. Anna Giraud was in Graz in 1739–40 and may have prepared the ground, but Vivaldi obviously hoped that Emperor Charles VI would remember his once illustrious dedicator. In 1740, after complicated negotiations, Vivaldi sold a large collection of his concertos and religious music to the Pietà (this is now, after many vicissitudes, a precious legacy of the Turin National Library), and left Italy for the last time.

Vivaldi went to Vienna, but Charles VI, his great hope, died. We know nothing of Vivaldi's life in the Imperial and Royal capital, he made little or no mark. He was old, forgotten and ill; there, in penury, he died 'of internal

Theatres proliferated in 18th-century Venice, but none of them survives (though the Fenice was rebuilt). The Teatro S. Samuele (OPPOSITE) was among the largest and best-equipped; the sets shown here are by Antonio Codagnato. LEFT Carlo Goldoni, who supplied libretti for operas as well as writing comedies. ABOVE the florid style of 18th-century vocal writing had its detractors. This brilliant cartoon of the singer Antonio Bernacchi represents his colaratura aria soaring over the top of the Campanile, coming down onto the Ducal Palace and ending in a trill.

inflammation' in July 1741. He was buried in the (now no longer extant) cemetery of the Bürgerspital. At his last rites the six choirboys of the great Cathedral in Vienna, St Stephen's, including the young Joseph Haydn, sang his Requiem Mass. No trace of his grave remains and Vivaldi's bones lie somewhere under the great Austrian capital, unmarked, about a mile from Mozart's.

Shameful though Vivaldi's worldly end had been and complete as was his subsequent disappearance from the world of music, his comeback was, after Monteverdi's, the most spectacular in the history of music. From tentative beginnings in the 19th century, Italian scholars, foremost among them Gian Francesco Malipiero, the well-known composer, made a concerted effort to resurrect Vivaldi and, incidentally, Monteverdi as well.

In 1939, there was a historic series of concerts at the Palazzo Chigi in Siena at which Vivaldi's operatic, religious and instrumental music was presented to a delighted and astonished public. (The next year the festival was devoted to the Scarlattis). After the war, the great Milanese house of Ricordi began to publish all the instrumental works of Vivaldi, mostly from the manuscripts in the Turin Library, and twenty-five years later that monumental project was complete; to be followed by a large selection of the great religious music, then almost all still unpublished. The marvelling world heard the magic sounds of the Motet 'Nisi Dominus', the Kyrie in D minor for double choir, the now famous Gloria in D (there are actually several), for the first time in over two hundred years. The *Four Seasons* became Number One on the best-selling gramophone record lists in England, and remained there for months on end. *Il prete rosso* became a household name on five continents.[16]

*   *   *

The most distinguished of all 18th-century musical visitors
to Venice was the young George Frederick Handel
(RIGHT), who was prevailed upon to write an opera for
the city in 1709. He wrote Agrippina in three weeks,
but only by plundering music from his other compositions,
including the oratorio La Resurrezione, of which the
autograph has survived (BELOW).

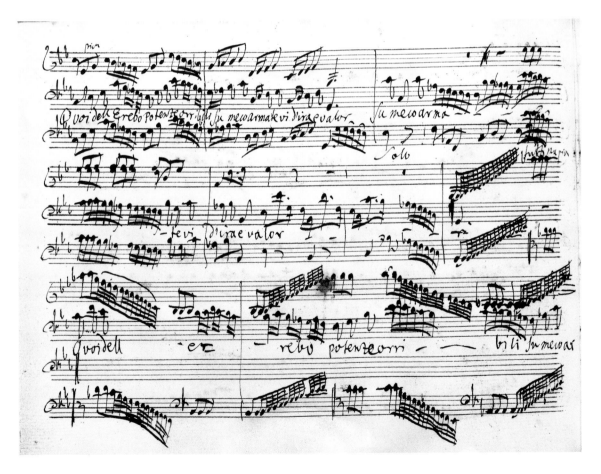

Domenico Scarlatti was in Venice at the time of Handel's visit, and it was he who recognized 'the famous Saxon' from the quality of his harpsichord playing, even though he was wearing a Carnival mask.

Baldassare Galuppi, born on the island of Burano, was maestro di coro at the Mendicanti and wrote a whole series of operas to libretti by Goldoni. The most popular was Il Filosofo di Campagna, dedicated 'to the most excellent ladies of Venice.'

IL FILOSOFO
DI
CAMPAGNA
DRAMMA GIOCOSO PER MUSICA
DI POLISSENO FEGEJO
PASTOR ARCADE
DA RAPPRESENTARSI
NEL TEATRO GRIMANI
DI S. SAMUEL
L'AUTUNNO dell' ANNO 1754.
Dedicato all' Eccellentissime
DAME VENEZIANE.

IN VENEZIA, MDCCLIV
PRESSO MODESTO FENZO.
Con Licenza de' Superiori

In 1709, the year Vivaldi was dismissed for the first time from the Pietà, another great Saxon composer, Handel, visited Venice as part of his tour of Italy. John Mainwaring, his first biographer, tells us:

It was his resolution to visit every part of Italy, which was any way famous for its musical performances. Venice was his next resort. He was first discovered there at a Masquerade, while he was playing on a harpsichord in his visor. [Domenico] SCARLATTI happened to be there, and affirmed that it could be no one but the famous Saxon, or the devil. Being thus detected, he was strongly importuned to compose an Opera. But there was so little prospect of either honour or advantage from such an undertaking, that he was very unwilling to engage in it . . .

At last, however, he consented, and in three weeks he finished his AGRIPPINA (in 1709), which was performed twenty-seven nights successively; and in a theatre which had been shut up for a long time, notwithstanding there were two other Opera-houses open at the same time; at one of which GASPARINI presided, as LOTTI did at the other. The audience was so enchanted with this performance, that a stranger who should have seen the manner in which they were affected, would have imagined they had all been distracted.

The theatre, at almost every pause, resounded with shouts and acclamations of 'viva il caro Sassone!' and other expressions of approbation too extravagant to be mentioned. They were thunderstruck with the grandeur and sublimity of his style: for never had they known till then all the powers of harmony and modulation so closely arrayed, and so forcibly combined.

This Opera drew over all the best singers from the other houses. Among the foremost of these was the famous VITTORIA, who a little before Handel's removal to Venice had obtained permission of the grand Duke [of Tuscany] to sing in one of the houses there. At AGRIPPINA her inclinations gave new lustre to her talents. Handel seemed almost as great and majestic as APOLLO, and it was far from the lady's intention to be so cruel and obstinate as DAPHNE.[17]

The first performance of *Agrippina* was given on 26 December 1709. The enthusiasm with which the opera was received demonstrates that it did not suffer from the great speed at which it was written. Handel was always a swift worker, but even so the composition of a full-length *opera seria* within three weeks was only made possible by heavy borrowing from other works not yet heard in Venice. This was considered a perfectly legitimate practice. *Opera seria* in those days was composed at great speed, revised quickly and subject to a variety of last-minute substitutions that required composers to be expert pragmatists. Composers not only borrowed from their own works, but also from those of their colleagues, and it was even normal for singers to insert their favourite aria into productions of different operas.

Handel's brief visit to Venice was a foretaste of what was to come in the 19th century. With Vivaldi's death Venice lost its last great composer. One, Baldassare Galuppi (1706–85), made a name for himself composing operas to libretti by the renowned playwright, Carlo Goldini; but Galuppi's music is not much peformed today. From the end of the 18th century onwards Venice's greatest musical achievement was the provision of inspiration to visiting composers.

IV   The Nineteenth Century

*T*he 19th century was the saddest in Venetian history. The Most Serene Republic was finished – and the Venetians, looking back on the manner of its end, felt not only grief but shame, knowing full well that they had not lifted a finger to save it. For the first time, they found themselves not only a subject race but an unwanted one – for Napoleon, having conquered the Veneto, after only five months handed it over to Austria. Returned to France for nine years from 1805, it became Austrian again in 1814 and remained so for the next half century. (A heroic attempt in the 'revolution year' of 1848 to throw off the Hapsburg yoke enabled Daniele Manin and his followers to proclaim the rebirth of the old Republic, but it lasted little more than a year before being crushed.) Only in 1866, with the Risorgimento and the Unification of Italy, did Venice regain her self-respect as an integral part of the new Italian state; but her independence was gone for ever. Most of us tend to see the Venice of the ottocento *less through the eyes of her own people than through those of foreign writers and painters – whom she inspired as she always had, and no longer by her beauty alone; for there was now a romantic sense of melancholy and decay, of greatness past and pleasures flown, that accorded perfectly with the spirit of the age.*

Of these visitors, none responded more characteristically to that inspiration than George Gordon, Lord Byron. Whether furnishing the Palazzo Mocenigo, effortlessly tossing off stanza after stanza of Don Juan, *learning Armenian in the monastery of S. Lazzaro or endeavouring to pacify one or the other of his furiously jealous mistresses, Byron in Venice is somehow always at his most Byronic – and wonderfully unlike the next of his great compatriots to surrender to the Venetian spell and make the city his second home, John Ruskin. Few people read* The Stones of Venice *today – and not surprisingly either, since it is interminably long, impossibly detailed and impenetrably organized. But for those of us who are not embarrassed by purple patches the book contains some of the finest and most perceptive writing in the English language, while for those of us who can never read enough about Venice it remains the most majestic ever to have been written on the city.*

We have to wait until the final decades of the century before there appears a novelist who instinctively responds to Venice as whole-heartedly as Byron and Ruskin had done; and that novelist is Henry James. The Aspern Papers *and, even more,* The Wings of the Dove *are permeated by the city on every page; here, as well as in his travel book* Italian Hours *and his incomparable letters, are descriptions that have never been bettered: descriptions not so much of the art and architecture as of the mists, and the magic, and the changing light; descriptions, in short, as instantly evocative of the essential Venice as is the work of J.M.W. Turner, the only painter of the century – apart, arguably, from Claude Monet – with courage and vision enough to meet, triumphantly, the Venetian challenge.*

36　*Venice may not have changed, but our ways of perceiving it have. The 19th century's Venice was not the 18th century's, nor the 17th's. It was more sombre, more melancholy, more steeped in the poetry of the past. This vision of the city, present in the work of, for instance, Ruskin and Turner, may be said to have culminated in Thomas Mann's* Death in Venice, *published in 1913. The view opposite, looking along the Grand Canal to S. Maria della Salute, is part of that vision, Venice seen through northern eyes. It was painted by the Russian artist Aleksandr Mordvinov, who died in 1858.*

And so, finally, to the greatest English poet of Venice. Robert Browning paid several visits to the city he loved, and – like Richard Wagner – paid it the ultimate compliment of dying there, on the mezzanine floor of the Cà Rezzonico on 12 December 1889. He wrote, to my knowledge, only three poems about the city. Two are good – very good – but one is a masterpiece, probably the finest poem ever written on the subject in any language; and as it claims to have been inspired by one of Venice's leading composers, it is surely only right that as much of it as space allows should be included in this book.

A TOCCATA OF GALUPPI'S

Oh Galuppi, Baldassaro, this is very sad to find!
I can hardly misconceive you; it would prove me deaf and blind;
But although I take your meaning, 'tis with such a heavy mind!

Here you come with your old music, and here's all the good it brings.
What, they lived once thus at Venice where the merchants were the kings,
Where St Mark's is, where the Doges used to wed the sea with rings? . . .

Did young people take their pleasure when the sea was warm in May?
Balls and masks begun at midnight, burning ever to mid-day,
When they made up fresh adventures for the morrow, do you say? . . .

Well, and it was graceful of them – they'd break talk off and afford
– She, to bite her mask's black velvet – he, to finger on his sword,
While you sat and played Toccatas, stately at the clavichord.

What? Those lesser thirds so plaintive, sixths diminished, sigh on sigh,
Told them something? Those suspensions, those solutions – 'Must we die?'
Those commiserating sevenths – 'Life might last! we can but try!'

'Were you happy?' – 'Yes.' – 'And are you still as happy?' – Yes. And you?'
Then, more kisses! – Did I stop them, when a million seemed so few?
Hark, the dominant's persistence till it must be answered to!

So, an octave struck the answer. Oh, they praised you, I dare say!
'Brave Galuppi! that was music! good alike at grave and gay!
'I can always leave off talking when I hear a master play!'

Then they left you for their pleasure: till in due time, one by one,
Some with lives that came to nothing, some with deeds as well undone,
Death stepped tacitly and took them where they never see the sun.

But when I sit down to reason, think to take my stand nor swerve,
While I triumph o'er a secret wrung from nature's close reserve,
In you come with your cold music till I creep thro' every nerve.

Yes, you, like a ghostly cricket, creaking where a house was burned:
'Dust and ashes, dead and done with, Venice spent what Venice earned.
'The soul, doubtless, is immortal – where a soul can be discerned . . .

'As for Venice and her people, merely born to bloom and drop,
'Here on earth they bore their fruitage, mirth and folly were the crop:
'What of soul was left, I wonder, when the kissing had to stop?

'Dust and ashes!' So you creak it, and I want the heart to scold.
Dear dead women, with such hair too – what's become of all the gold
Used to hang and brush their bosoms? I feel chilly and grown old.

Opera was the dominant musical form of 19th-century Italy, occupying the talents of all her great composers and giving singers that immense popularity and prestige they still enjoy. Not that their lives were always easy. They were overworked; their contracts with managements could be enforced if necessary by the police, however ill they were feeling; and their voices seldom lasted beyond early middle age.

37, 38, 39 *La Fenice* (ABOVE LEFT) *had been built in the great days of the Republic, when it was merely the largest of several flourishing opera houses in Venice. It is now the sole survivor, rebuilt and somewhat altered. This view concentrates on the audience rather than the performance. There is no separate orchestra pit; the players sit in front of the stage, directed from the keyboard or the first violin. Two armed soldiers are in attendance to keep order and discourage political demonstrations. The fashionable spectators occupy the boxes, the backs of which could be screened off to make virtually private rooms for dining or for any other purpose that might be desired.*
ABOVE *the prison scene from Rossini's* Tancredi, *the set (an odd mixture of Gothic vaulting and classical frieze) designed by Sanquirico.*
LEFT *a fan with a portrait of Rossini and six characters from his operas:* Tancredi, The Thieving Magpie, Otello, The Barber of Seville, The Lady of the Lake *and* Armida.

40, 41   *Fashion and wealth returned to Venice after the city became part of an independent Italy in 1866. Michele Cammarano's painting of 1869 shows the Piazza San Marco bustling with night life.*

But the crowd is now cosmopolitan and on holiday, rather than native Venetian.
INSET: *Florian's, still the best café on the Piazza and little changed since the 1860s.*

HERNANI
ACTE 2ᵉ SCÈNE 11ᵉ

42   Aida *at La Fenice: the poster for Verdi's most spectacular grand opera combines as many ancient Egyptian motifs as possible, even the title being made up of posturing human figures.*

43, 44   *Verdi's three triumphs in Venice were* Ernani *(1844),* Rigoletto *(1851) and, after a false start,* La Traviata *(1854).* Ernani (INSET) *was based on a play by Victor Hugo. Here Elvira, about to be married to her uncle, Don Silva, discovers that a beggar just admitted to the castle is in fact her lover Ernani, whom she believed dead. Silva comes upon them as they swear eternal love.* Rigoletto *was also an adaptation of a Victor Hugo play,* Le roi s'amuse. *Bertoja's set for the second scene of Act I* (LEFT) *shows the street in Mantua with Rigoletto's house on the left, where he keeps his beloved daughter Gilda.*

During the 16th, 17th and 18th centuries, Venice was gradually slipping into political and economic decline. The Venetians compensated for this decline by spending increasing sums on art, architecture and music. The Serenissima staged many grand public ceremonies each year, all of which required new pieces of music to be written. At the beginning of the 19th century Venice surrendered her independence to France and then Austria. Under foreign rule, no money was available for the arts and there was no state demand for new music. Without the Serenissima actively encouraging new art, architecture and music, Venice became a museum. In the 19th century Venice ceased to create anything new herself, but inspired art and music in visitors.

Benjamin Disraeli put it in this way:

If I were to assign the particular quality which conduces to that dreamy and voluptuous existence which men of high imagination experience in Venice, I should describe it as the feeling of abstraction which is remarkable in that city and peculiar to it. Venice is the only city which can yield the magical delights of solitude. All is still and silent. No rude sound disturbs your reveries; fancy, therefore, is not put to flight. No rude sound distracts your self-consciousness. This renders existence intense. We feel everything. And we feel thus keenly in a city not only eminently beautiful, not only abounding in wonderful creations of art, but each step of which is hallowed ground, quick with associations that, in their more various nature, their nearer relation to ourselves, and perhaps their more picturesque character, exercise a greater influence over the imagination than the more antique story of Greece and Rome.[1]

In 1796 Napoleon arrived in northern Italy at the head of the French revolutionary armies. The following year Venice was invaded for the first time in her history by foreign troops. Napoleon issued an ultimatum – 'I want no more Inquisition, no more Senate, I shall be an Attila to Venice'.[2] Thus, the Serenissima, the oldest republic in Europe, ceased to exist, abandoning power to the French.

William Wordsworth commemorated this event in a sonnet:

> Once did She hold the gorgeous east in fee;
>   And was the safeguard of the west: the worth
>   Of Venice did not fall below her birth,
> Venice, the eldest Child of Liberty.
> She was a maiden City, bright and free;
>   No guile seduced, no force could violate;
>   And, when she took unto herself a Mate,
> She must espouse the everlasting Sea.

45 *The funeral gondola gives death in Venice a special touch of romantic grandeur. Thus Wagner's body began the first stage of its journey back to Bayreuth. Thus Igor Stravinsky was conveyed to rest on the cemetery island of S. Michele.*

Napoleon entered Italy with a
revolutionary army in 1796.
Provoked by an attack on a
French ship and the killing of
its commander, he demanded the
surrender of Venice and the
abolition of the republic. On
May 12 the Great Council was
disbanded. A fortnight later the
French were in possession of the
city, and one of their first acts
was to take down the Horses of
San Marco (OPPOSITE) and
remove them to Paris, where
they remained until 1815.

> And what if she had seen those glories fade,
> Those titles vanish, and that strength decay;
>   Yet shall some tribute of regret be paid
> When her long life hath reached its final day:
>   Men are we, and must grieve when even the Shade
> Of that which once was great, is passed away.[3]

After being passed between France and Austria like the pawn she now was, Venice was ceded to the Austrian Empire in 1815. Venice fell on evil times. The once proud citizens bowed under the severe Austrian rule; women who were caught uttering anti-Austrian statements were stripped to the waist and flogged in the squares; and as their screams subsided, salt was flung on their raw and bleeding backs. The Austrian censors exercised iron control over the theatres; all the libretti were read for anti-establishment tendencies. Anything anti-royal, anti-aristocrat, pro-Republican was forbidden. The spoken theatre and the opera became dull and insipid. Society was frivolous and ill-read; there was hardly anything interesting to read and the only kind of plays the Austrians allowed wholeheartedly were Goldoni's.

The decadence of Venice [wrote Lady Frances Shelley] is due to the fact that it belongs to Austria. Every encouragement is now given to Trieste, while trade was completely shackled in the time of the French. The Arsenal alone employed six thousand people in the old days. It now scarcely employs as many hundreds. There is now no Court, or centre of Government, which, in the time of the Doges, gave life and industry to every branch of trade in Venice . . . Ancient costumes and customs are neglected. The clocks no longer strike twenty-four hours; and, in consequence, all the hours are alike. The theatre begins at nine o'clock and the casino at twelve.[4]

Lord Byron came to Venice in 1816. Here he mourns its degradation under foreign rule:

> The spouseless Adriatic mourns her lord;
>   And, annual marriage now no more renew'd,
> The Bucentaur lies rotting unrestored,
>   Neglected garment of her widowhood!
>   St Mark yet sees his lion where he stood
> Stand, but in mockery of his wither'd power,
>   Over the proud Place where an Emperor sued,
> And monarchs gazed and envied in the hour
> When Venice was a queen with an unequall'd dower.
>
> Before St Mark still glow his steeds of brass,
>   Their gilded collars glittering in the sun;
> But is not Doria's menace come to pass?
>   Are they not bridled? — Venice, lost and won,
>   Her thirteen hundred years of freedom done,
> Sinks, like a seaweed, unto whence she rose!
>   Better be whelm'd beneath the waves, and shun,
> Even in destruction's depth, her foreign foes,
> From whom submission wrings an infamous repose.[5]

Byron came to Venice late in 1816. His first lodging was at a house in the Frezzeria (FAR LEFT), a narrow street just off the Piazza San Marco, kept by a draper called Segati. Here he made himself at home by starting a love affair with his landlord's wife. 'She is in her twenty-second year. Marianna (that is her name) is in her appearance altogether like an antelope. She has large, black, oriental eyes . . .'

Early in 1818 (the sale of Newstead Abbey having made him £95,000 richer) Byron moved into the huge Palazzo Mocenigo on the Grand Canal (RIGHT, in 1830 and today; it is the one with the tall chimneys, on the left in the modern photograph). Here Marianna was supplanted by a baker's wife (hence called 'La Fornarina') and later by his last, most serious and most permanent mistress Teresa Guiccioli. In the vast rooms of the Mocenigo (LEFT) Byron lived a somewhat disordered life with 'about fourteen servants', numerous dogs and birds and a fox. Here he wrote the first two cantos of Don Juan.

Shelley too, partisan of liberty and enemy of tyrants everywhere, detested the Venetian submission to foreign rule. In a letter to a friend in 1818, he explains this:

Venice, which was once a tyrant, is now the next worse thing, a slave; for in fact it ceased to be free or worth our regret as a nation, from the moment that the oligarchy usurped the rights of the people. Yet, I do not imagine that it was ever so degraded as it has been since the French, and especially the Austrian yoke. The Austrians take sixty per cent in taxes, and impose free quarters on the inhabitants. A horde of German soldiers, as vicious and more disgusting than the Venetians themselves, insult these miserable people. I had no conception of the excess to which avarice, cowardice, superstition, ignorance, passionless lust, and all the inexpressible brutalities which degrade human nature, could be carried until I had passed a few days at Venice.[6]

Despite the strain of foreign oppression and the malaise of Venetian citizens, everyday life continued. The reputation of Venetian women was changing in the 19th century, they became better known for their gentility, rather than as in past centuries when they had been known for their beauty and their libertine ways.

A Venetian lady's day is thus passed. She rises about 12 o'clock when the cavalier servente who waits until she is awake, attends her to Mass. Few of them read anything except their prayer books. The lady then takes a few turns on the Piazza San Marco, either pays visits or receives them, and dines between 3 and 4 o'clock. She then undresses and goes to bed completely. At about 8 o'clock she arises for her toilette, spends until 3 or 4 o'clock in the morning at the theatre and the casino, or during the summer, in the cafes on the Piazza.[7]

There were generally three or four seasons of opera a year of which the most celebrated was the one known as the Carnival, beginning on Boxing Day, 26 December. Ever since Monteverdi's time, when Venice had been the host to the first public opera house, they had fulfilled a unique function in Italian life. The public theatres were run by impresarios who expected to make a handsome profit and very often did. Theatres were the principal meeting place for people of all classes: one could gamble at ridotto rooms; dine in pleasant public rooms or in the privacy of a box; or play cards if you were bored with the recitatives. A successful opera would play every night for weeks on end and the same audience would return each night. At times the audience might not even be listening to the opera, following instead the dramas that occurred off-stage. Lord Byron and Countess Teresa Guiccioli had begun an affair in 1819. When Teresa was informed by her husband that they were to leave the city, she rushed immediately to find Byron at the opera house, she 'almost involuntarily followed him into his box and told him of her troubles. This box was generally used by men only, and was always the target of Venetian curiosity. One can imagine that this was increased a hundredfold by the young lady's presence!'[8] But the Italian public took their opera very seriously, woe betide if they were bored or if the singer performed his part badly, they would be booed off stage.

Venetian theatres contained public rooms, cafés and gambling tables. The foyer of the Teatro Gallo (BELOW) was a large, classically-proportioned space, leading at the back into the auditorium and up the stairs to the boxes. On the right is a spacious bar.

In 1836 a disastrous fire destroyed Venice's opera house, La Fenice, built in 1791 to the design of Giananto nio Selva.

With their wooden construction, candles and gas jets, a common fate for theatres was destruction by fire. In 1836 the beautiful 18th-century Teatro La Fenice which had opened with an opera by the veteran settecento composer, Giovanni Paisiello, in 1792, burnt down. It was, of course, immediately rebuilt, reopening a year later. This structure remains one of the sights of Venice today, with very few changes. It became the symbol of all the famous and beautiful opera houses of Venice which gradually disappeared during the 19th and 20th centuries, eventually leaving the Fenice, rich in tradition, in undisputed sway.

The collapse of Venetian musical life was seen at first hand by the composer Spohr:

We were visited today by a German musician, Aiblinger, a native of Munich and a pupil of Winter, who has been living in Venice for sixteen years. He is a pianist and composer and seems to have a real feeling for his art. At least, he complained, almost with tears in his eyes, that in this country [Italy] he was deprived of any opportunity of keeping pace with his German musical contemporaries. He almost never had the fortune to hear an important German work, and it simply broke his heart to be bound by his fate to a city where for 16 years, the same music was played over and over again, while the Germans, in the same space of time, had produced many a classic. He knows our newer music quite imperfectly from piano scores which he manages to procure from time to time at great expense of money and effort. I have subsequently had a look at his work and can testify

that he might have amounted to something if he had not been couped up in this artistic Siberia.[9]

It was a poor time for Italian music but Venetian life continued in its own inimitable way. Spohr did discover that there was a Venetian musical life of sorts:

There are two series of amateur concerts here. One series under the direction of Count Tomasini, offers a concert every two weeks at the Teatro Fenice. At the concert which I attended, Therese Sessi . . . sang two arias, a duet, and a quartet . . . In addition to her there was an amateur who sang a number of buffo pieces in the authentic, rather exaggerated Italian manner. Everything else, particularly the overture, as regards both composition and performance was, as usual in Italy, most wretched. The other is a mere rehearsal series which takes place every week under the direction of Contin. The orchestra, with the exception of the basses and a few winds, consists exclusively of amateurs. It devotes itself mostly to symphonies and overtures of German masters. One can hardly speak, however, of a serious study of these works. Just getting through without breaking down is reckoned quite a success. The day I was there they played first an ancient symphony by Krommer, followed by Romburg's Symphony in E flat. At the end I was asked to conduct Beethoven's Symphony No 2 in D which I could not very well refuse. It was an ordeal. The orchestra was accustomed to tempi quite different from mine, and seemed unaware of the existence of distinctions between loud and soft. Everyone scraped and blew for all he was worth. The noise was such that my ears ached

'La Fenice' means The Phoenix, and it was so called because it had risen from its ashes. After 1836 it proved its name once more. The auditorium was restored as it had been (ABOVE), though later – in 1856 and again in this century – it was redecorated and made more Rococo than it had ever been before.

The gondola entrance to La Fenice was where the fashionable audience would arrive, and this entrance is still used today (OPPOSITE).

all night. These concerts have the virtue of acquainting the Venetian music lovers with our classical instrumental music, such as the overtures to Don Giovanni and the Magic Flute. Thus they can sense, if dimly, that the Germans in this field are immeasurably superior to the Italians. They admit this, to be sure, but don't really believe it, and say it only in order that they may then emphasise, without embarassment, their own superiority in singing and in vocal composition! The smugness of the Italians, in conjunction with the paucity of their own production is sheerly intolerable. When I played one of my own compositions they knew no higher praise than to assure me that it was to the Italian taste.[10]

Felix Mendelssohn visited Venice in 1830; however, he found more inspiration in the city's art than in music:

I do not regret that I have heard scarcely any music here as yet; for I suppose I must not include the music of the angels in the 'Assumption', encircling Mary with joyous shouts of welcome, one gaily beating the tambourine, a couple of others blowing away on strange crooked flutes, whilst another charming group is singing – or the music floating in the thoughts of the player. I have only once heard anything on the organ, and that was doleful. I was gazing at Titian's 'Martyrdom of St Peter' in the Franciscan Church. Divine service was going on, and nothing inspires me with more solemn awe than when on the very spot for which they were originally designed and painted, those old pictures with their mighty figures, gradually steal forth out of the darkness in which the long lapse of time has veiled them.[11]

In 1848 Venice, in common with other nations in Europe, rose against her foreign oppressors and for a few months the ancient Republic was restored. But blockade, bombardment, starvation and disease finally forced the city to surrender.

In the 1840s, in reaction to this degradation, the 'Risorgimento', a movement for Italian national unity and independence, began to gain strength. This time their leaders were men of the middle classes – professional men, lawyers, academics and soldiers. In 1848 half of Europe rebelled against Vienna. As news of these uprisings reached Venice, her citizens rose in arms too, spurring their own insurrection. In March, Daniele Manin officially proclaimed the new Republic of Venice:

We are free, and we have a double right to boast of it because we have become free without shedding a drop of blood, either our own or our brothers, for I call all men brothers. But it is not enough to have overthrown the old Government; we must put another in its place. The right one, I think, is the republic. It will remind us of our past glories improved by modern liberties. We do not thereby mean to separate ourselves from our Italian brothers. Rather we will form one of those centres which must bring about the gradual fusion of Italy into one. Viva la repubblica! Viva Libertà! Viva San Marco![12]

For a full year the cause was hopeless. The Austrians blocked the lagoon and bombarded the city. Provisions ran desperately short. Cholera broke out. Without foreign help the Venetians hardly stood a chance. But they resisted longer than any of the other rebellious Italian cities. In August 1849, the desperate Venetians surrendered and the Austrians reoccupied the city.

Venice subsided into sullen thralldom, boycotting everything Austrian, even the military band in the Piazza. William Dean Howells (US Consul in Venice in the 1860s) observed the unyielding hostility between imperious Austrians and rebellious Venetians:

... As the social life of Italy, and especially of Venice, was in great part to be once enjoyed at the theatres, at the caffe, and at the other places of public resort, so is its absence now to be chiefly noted in those places. No lady of perfect standing among her people goes to the opera, and the men never go in the boxes, but if they frequent the theatre at all, they take places in the pit, in order that the house may wear as empty and dispirited a look as possible.... In regard to the caffe, there is a perfectly understood system by which the Austrians go to one, and the Italians to another: and Florian's, in the Piazza, seems to be the only common ground in the city on which the hostile forces consent to meet. This is because it is thronged with foreigners of all nations, and to go there is not thought a demonstration of any kind ... It is in the Piazza that the tacit demonstration of hatred and discontent chiefly takes place. Here, thrice a week, in winter and summer, the military band plays that exquisite music for which the Austrians are famous. The selections are usually from Italian operas, and the attraction is the hardest of all others for the music-loving Italian to resist. But he does resist it. There are some noble ladies who have not entered the Piazza while the band was playing there, since the fall of the Republic of 1849 ... they pass from the Piazza when the music begins, and walk upon the long quay at the sea-side of the Ducal Palace; or if they remain in the Piazza they pace up and down under the arcades on either side; for Venetian patriotism makes a delicate distinction between listening to the Austrian band in the Piazza and hearing it under the Procuratie, forbidding the first and permitting the last. As soon as the music ceases the Austrians disappear, and the Italians return to the Piazza.[13]

Italy became an independent kingdom in 1861; Venice had to wait another five years before being liberated from Austrian rule – an event put onto the Venetian stage with characteristic brio (OPPOSITE).

After the Austro-Prussian war, Venice at last secured her freedom, joining the newly formed Kingdom of Italy in 1866.

When the railway came to Venice she lost her unique status and something of her magic. Now more than ever she became a museum for tourists. But if the railway impoverished Venice's character as a living city, it probably enriched it as a musical centre.

But during those seven decades of servitude, the inner life had disappeared from Venice. It had lost its raison d'être: music and art had been subject to censorship, her citizens had been oppressed and the commercial pulse of the city had fled across the lagoon to the abominable factories and harbours of Mestre. The Industrial Revolution was now to cement Venice's downfall. In the manner of all revolutions, Mestre began to consume its own father. Mark Twain wrote:

This Venice, which was a haughty, invincible, magnificent Republic for nearly fourteen hundred years; whose armies compelled the world's applause whenever and wherever they battled; whose navies well nigh held dominion of the seas, and whose merchant fleets whitened the remotest oceans with their sails and loaded these piers with the products of every clime, is fallen a prey to poverty, neglect and melancholy decay. Six hundred years ago, Venice was the Autocrat of Commerce; her mart was the great commercial centre, the distributing house from whence the enormous trade of the Orient was spread abroad over the Western world. Today her piers are deserted, her warehouses are empty, her merchant fleets are vanished, her armies and her navies are but memories. Her glory is departed, and with her crumbling grandeur of wharves and palaces about her she sits among her stagnant lagoons, forlorn and beggared, forgotten of the world. She that in her palmy days commanded the commerce of a hemisphere and made the weal or woe of the peoples of the earth, – a peddler of glass beads for women, and trifling toys and trinkets for school-girls and children.[14]

Following her economic decline, and having lost her independence, she had become a glorious museum for tourists, holding an attraction for travellers from all over the world. One of them was Henry James:

There are travellers who think the place odious, and those who are not of this opinion often find themselves wishing that the others were only more numerous. The sentimental tourist's sole quarrel with his Venice is that he has too many competitors there. He likes to be alone; to be original; to have (to himself, at least) the air of making discoveries. The Venice of today is a vast museum where the little wicket that admits you is perpetually turning and creaking, and you march through the institution with a herd of fellow-gazers . . . But this is not the fault of Venice; it is the fault of the rest of the world . . .[15]

To this story of cultural decline there is one glorious exception – opera. And it is upon opera rather than on other forms of music that we must concentrate during the 19th century. This would not be the case if we were discussing music anywhere else; in Austria, France, Germany or England. It is no accident that the great late German symphonists, Brahms, Bruckner and Mahler, wrote no operas and equally significant that Giuseppe Verdi wrote only one major non-operatic composition – the String Quartet for an amateur society in Naples.

Tourists came to Venice in search of the past. Its air of decay was a source of pleasure, as it had been for Byron. Increasingly it was seen through the eyes of Romanticism.

Fanny Tacchinardi-Persiani, whose singing in Rossini's Tancredi *in 1813 helped to make it a success.* Tancredi *was a more tragic work than Rossini's earlier operas and established him as a serious composer.*

Musical life in Italy was coming to mean almost exclusively opera. Who can name one significant Italian symphony of the 19th century? The principal protagonists of music in 19th-century Venice – Rossini, Verdi, Tchaikovsky and Wagner – were non Venetians. Gone were the days when Venice herself and her native sons were at the centre of musical activities. Venice was becoming also a musical museum. To follow the development of opera as a connected story, we have to return to the years following the collapse of the Republic, when Venice was under French rule.

In those days operas were presented very differently from the way they are to-day. The historian Julian Budden describes it thus:

The stage had a large proscenium area which projected about four metres into the auditorium. There was no orchestral pit; the players were simply strung in front of the footlights; and there were no professional conductors until after 1860 or thereabouts. The performances were directed by the *primo violino* using his bow to give the beat for the first few bars of each piece and then joining in himself. Each opera was played towards the box-holders (the audience in the stalls hardly counted), and therefore all the pieces of importance, whether arias or ensembles, were normally delivered from the footlights. This explains why in Verdi and Rossini there are so many of those arias with a text written, as it were, in parentheses, which the other characters on stage, including the chorus, are not supposed to hear. And of course it was essential to capture the attention of the people in the boxes, otherwise they would happily continue chatting amongst themselves. They could even play cards if they were bored since the houselights were never lowered. For the first three performances of a new opera the composer himself was expected to be present in the orchestra (he usually sat by the keyboard, if the opera required one for the recitatives, otherwise by the leading double-bass player) and if a piece was liked it would be applauded there and then, there would be cries of 'Fuori Maestro!' and he would have to walk on to the stage and take a bow with the singers.

Of course, during the latter part of the century opera became less of an essentially aristocratic entertainment and all this began to change. The proscenium was cut back in order to accommodate an increasing number of stall-holders whose contribution was now becoming important to the box-office. The orchestra had to be lowered into a pit so as to allow everyone an uninterrupted view of the stage. As scores grew more complicated and continuous, with fewer breaks for applause, so the professional conductor arose who took charge of every aspect of the musical performance. Candles gave way to oil-lamps, then to gaslight and finally, during the 1880s to electricity, after which the darkened auditorium became the rule. But it needed Toscanini to put an end to the demand for encores.

For the singers, life was far harder in Verdi's time than it is today. Often they were required to perform night after night and then to undertake long uncomfortable journeys by stage-coach to another theatre. If they felt unwell and the impresario didn't believe them he would send round a police officer to their lodgings who would drag them to the theatre. One result of this is that careers tended to be much shorter than they are to-day. Giuseppina Strepponi, Verdi's second wife, was a genuine star; but she was finished before she was thirty.

The century was only ten years old when Gioacchino Rossini arrived on the Venetian scene. 'Extremely good looking as a young man, he was always, even in his most tender years, a favourite among women of every class. They found his fresh complexion, his brown saucy eyes, his delicate hands and, above all, his winning, roguish smile almost irresistible.'[16]

During the autumn season of 1810 the impresario at the San Mosè theatre discovered that one of the composers had failed to deliver a new opera he had been engaged to write. A reportedly gifted but as yet untried composer was recommended. Rossini, then working in Bologna, was asked by letter if he would like to compose it. His answer was to rush immediately to Venice. The eighteen-year-old was handed his new libretto entitled *La cambiale di matrimonio* (Marriage by Promissory Note) and set it to music in just a few days. The rehearsals went

FILIPPO GALLI *nella Semiramide*.

The bass Filippo Galli in Rossini's Semiramide, *Venice 1823. After the relative failure of* Maometto, *this opera restored Rossini's standing. It ran for twenty-eight nights to rapturous applause.*

badly, but one of the singers helped Rossini with the practicalities: in the 18th and early 19th centuries producing and composing operas was always very much a pragmatic affair, but Rossini learned quickly. On 3 November 1810 *La cambiale di matrimonio* took Venice by storm. The libretto was not the best, a story of how a rich Canadian merchant tries, for commercial reasons, to marry the daughter of his English correspondent, but is obliged to renounce his claims in favour of a genuine love. Rossini made the best of it; his score is fresh and charming with some attractive arias. The principal and overwhelming characteristic of this, Rossini's debut in Venice, was its sense of fun and its irrepressible high spirits.

Rossini's first undiluted success was *L'inganno felice* (Fortunate Deception), produced at the San Mosè Theatre on 8 January 1812. 'The illiteracy of the press notices was equalled only by their enthusiasm, and the opera remained in the bill until the last night of the season, when, to mark their admiration for the work and the fine singing of the leading lady, some enthusiasts let loose in the theatre a bevy of doves, canaries and guinea fowl.'[17] When *La scala di seta* (The Silken Ladder) opened in the spring of 1812, it was unfavourably compared with *L'inganno felice*. For us in the 20th century, however, the overture with its early example of the famous Rossini *crescendo* is one of those irresistible acts of nature with which Italian music is frequently gifted.

Following the success of other operas in Milan, Rossini became a household name throughout Italy. He was commissioned to write several works in Venice, including an *opera seria* for La Fenice; this was to place Rossini ahead of all his Italian contemporaries. On 6 February 1813 Rossini broke the barriers once again with *Tancredi*. Based on a tragedy of that name by Voltaire, the plot is a romance, involving a misunderstanding between the hero and heroine, and is set during conflicts between Christians and Moslems. The Venetians went mad over it. One of the arias entitled '*Di tanti palpiti*' was the kind of success composers dream of: the gondoliers sang it in the morning, the waiters sang it in the coffee houses at noon and the aristocracy sang it in the evening. Even in courts of law people had to be ordered to stop humming the tune!

While *Tancredi* was genuinely popular, Rossini's next opera proved to be the most successful in Italy for a generation. *L'Italiana in Algeri*, written in less than a month, was first given at the San Benedetto Theatre on 22 May the same year: Rossini was just 21 years old. The libretto, based on the legend of the beautiful Roxelana, the favourite slave of Soliman the Second, tells the story of an Italian lady who, with the assistance of an admirer, sets out to rescue her lover. All the great former glories of Cimarosa, Paisiello, Haydn and Mozart, their tears, their laughter, their humanity, were poured into this magnificent score which, from the richly symphonic overture to the compulsive 'patter' finales, set a new standard for Italian opera and perhaps for music altogether.

Rossini lost popularity among the Venetian public after the dismal failure of *Maometto* in December 1822. His enemies suggested that he would not be able to write the new opera which had been commissioned by La Fenice, before the end of the season. Rossini confounded all his critics by writing *Semiramide*, an extremely long and complicated opera, in just 33 days. It opened on 3 February 1823. The libretto, adapted from another Voltaire tragedy, is the same story as Hamlet and Orestes, with the added twist that the guilty Queen mother falls in

love with her avenging son before discovering his identity; he then mistakes her for her lover and kills her.

Spoilt as the Venetians were by Rossini's excellent and civilized comedies and tragedies, an even greater operatic excitement was in store for them; the arrival of Italy's greatest opera composer, Giuseppe Verdi. He single-handedly brought about a radical change in Venetian theatrical life. The two masterpieces Verdi gave to Venice and the rest of the world, *Rigoletto* and *La Traviata*, are enough of an operatic feast to give Venice world fame even if no other composer had ever worked in the island city.

Before the middle of the century, Verdi had produced two operas at the Teatro La Fenice. Both were born with a certain amount of difficulty because of the Austrian censors, but Verdi eventually won out, allowing insignificant changes in names, titles and so on. *Ernani*, based on a subject of Victor Hugo's, opened in 1844. Two years later, Verdi fell ill, firstly with rheumatism and then gastric fever. Verdi later wrote that he completed his next opera, *Attila* 'in bed, in an almost dying condition'.[18] In the blood-curdling *Attila*, the Italians saw their most feared northern invaders, the Huns, swallowed up in the lagoons of their beloved city. The audience yelled, 'Italia, Italia!'. 'Attila has aroused real fanaticism; the Signor Maestro had every imaginable honour: wreaths, and a brass band with torches that accompanied him to his lodging, amid cheering crowds,'[19] wrote Verdi's pupil Emanuele Muzio.

Venice was also important to the career of the young Giuseppe Verdi. His first success there came when he was just over thirty, in 1844, when Ernani *was produced at La Fenice. The poster for the first performance tells us that the curtain will rise at 8 o'clock and that between Acts II and III there will be a ballet called* Nadir Shah of Persia. *Audiences of the 1840s demanded value for money.*

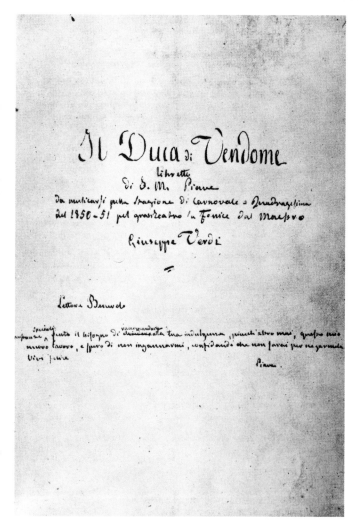

In 1851 Verdi wrote
Rigoletto, *an opera that marks
the beginning of his greatest
period and confirmed him as
Italy's leading opera composer.
Its triumph at La Fenice came
after a saga of setbacks and
battles with the censor.* ABOVE
*sketches of sets for the second
scene of Act I and Act IV by
G. and P. Bertoja.* ABOVE
RIGHT *poster for the first
performance.* RIGHT *at one
stage the opera was to be called*
Il Duca di Vendome – *the
setting was changed several times
to appease the censor.*
OPPOSITE *costume designs for*
Rigoletto, *the names of the
characters noted beneath.*

FIGURINI dell' Opera RIGOLETTO del Maestro G. VERDI

Gilda
Atto III Scena II e seguenti

Gilda
Atto III Scena I, II e III.

Gilda

Duca
Atto III Scena II e seguenti

Duca

Duca
in costume Borghese

Rigoletto
Atto I Scena III

Rigoletto
Atto I Scena VII

C.° di Monterone

Giovanna

C.° di Ceprano, Marullo, Borsa.
Coro e Ballerini (variando i Colori)

C.° di Ceprano
e Ballerine variando i Colori

Paggio
della Duchessa

Alabardieri Usciere C.° di Ceprano, Marullo Borsa,
e Coro (Colori variati)

Maddalena.

Sparafucile.

Paggi delle Dame
(Colori variati)

Servi di Corte.

Paggi del Duca.

MILANO
DALL' I. R. STABILIMENTO NAZIONALE PRIVILEGIATO DI
GIOVANNI RICORDI
Contrada degli Omenoni N. 1720, e sotto il portico a fianco dell' I. R. Teatro alla Scala.
incipre G. Ricordi e Jouhaud.

Following such a success it was natural that in 1850 the directors of La Fenice approached Verdi for a new opera for the next season. Verdi chose another tale by Victor Hugo, *Le Roi s'amuse*, and began working on it that autumn. In April he wrote to his librettist, Piave, about the project: 'I would have another subject which if the [Venice] police chose to allow it would be one of the greatest creations of modern theatre. Who knows? They allowed Ernani, they might allow this one too, and here there would be no conspiracies [A theme particularly disliked by the police who had real conspiracies to deal with at this time.] Try! the subject is great, immense, and there is a character in it who is one of the greatest creations of all countries and all periods . . . Tribolet.'[20] When Mazari, the President of the Fenice, heard about the subject (a frivolous and dissolute king, a loose girl who sleeps with him and a hideous hunchback) he was sure the censors would object seriously . . . and they did. They forbade the whole subject and wrote, viciously, that they 'deplored that [Verdi and his librettist] had not chosen another field in which to display their talents other than that of the repulsive immorality and obscene triviality which constitutes the argument of the piece entitled [as it was then] *La Maledizione*.'[21]

After receiving the censors' suggested changes, Verdi wrote the following letter to the theatre management, rejecting the changes and defending his original concept: 'Reduced in this way, it lacks character, importance, and finally the scenes have become very cold. If it was necessary to change the names, then the localities should also have been changed . . . The Duke is a nullity: the Duke must absolutely be a libertine; otherwise there is no justification for Triboletto's fear of his daughter's emerging from her hiding place; the drama becomes impossible. Why in the last Act, does the Duke go to a remote tavern alone, without an invitation, without an appointment?' In the final act, the heroine's body is delivered, by her murderer, to her father in a sack, to be thrown into the river. The censor had altered this scene too:

I do not understand why the sack has been omitted! What does the sack matter to the police? Are they afraid of the effect on stage? Then allow me to say: why do they claim to know more than I about this? Who is the Maestro? Who can say this will make an effect and this not? There was a similar problem about Ernani's horn: Well, who laughed at the sound of that horn? If the sack is omitted, it is unlikely that Triboletto would talk for half an hour to a corpse, before a flash of lightning comes to reveal that it is his daughter . . . Finally, I note that they have avoided making Triboletto ugly and a hunchback!! A hunchback who sings? Why not? . . . Will it be effective? I do not know. But, if I do not know, then neither, I repeat, does the person who has proposed this change. Actually I find it very beautiful to portray this character externally misshapen and ridiculous, but inwardly impassioned and full of love. I chose the subject precisely for these qualities and these original features. If they are removed, I cannot write the music. If I am told that my notes will work also for this drama, I reply that I do not understand this reasoning; and I will say frankly that my notes, ugly or beautiful as they may be, are never written at random and that I try always to give them a character . . . in short, an original, powerful drama has been turned into something quite banal and cold . . . In all conscience as an artist I cannot set this libretto to music.[22]

Eventually both sides made compromises. The piece was no longer called *The Curse* (frivolous and anti-church); the king (good heavens) was turned into the

Duke of Mantua; the hunchback Triboulet became, at first, Triboletto and then Rigoletto and the new title of the opera. Nevertheless *Rigoletto* was a revolution in opera. It was first given at La Fenice on 11 March 1851 and was an immediate success. Verdi himself realized what an innovation *Rigoletto* was; he wrote, 'ten years ago I would not have risked doing *Rigoletto*; today I would refuse to compose subjects of the kind like *Nabucco, I due Foscari* etc. They present most interesting moments on the stage, but without variety. It is one string, an elevated one if you will, but still always the same . . .'[23] *Rigoletto* was an international success, travelling to Austria, Budapest, Prague, Stuttgart, Lübeck, Bremen and England.

It might appear that Verdi's relationship with Venice was something of an interlude between his grand successes and grand failures elsewhere, in Milan and Rome, later in London and Paris, not to mention Vienna. This is not so; Verdi's many sojourns in the lagoon city turned out to be pivotal for him and the history of opera. On 6 March 1853, La Fenice was again the host for a new and important work by Verdi: *La Traviata*, based on Alexandre Dumas's *La Dame aux Camellias*. The composer was unwell while writing this opera, working in an atmosphere of gloom and foreboding.

La Fenice continued to serve as the major opera house of Venice throughout the 19th century – indeed as one of the major opera houses of the world. The entrance from the piazza, which survived the fire of 1836 unscathed, is modest in scale and gives no hint of the grandeur within.

La Traviata's *début* at La Fenice in 1853 was a disaster for which poor performance was to blame. But Venice redeemed itself a year later when it was revived at the Teatro San Benedetto and acclaimed a masterpiece. ABOVE a poster for the first night. It is still hard to imagine an audience, at the end of a performance of La Traviata, *wishing to sit through a five-act ballet called* The Magic Lantern. ABOVE RIGHT *Bertoja's sketch design for Act I.* BELOW RIGHT *the piano arrangement of the opera, with an illustration of the last act – Violetta dying, Alfredo stricken with grief, his father with remorse.* OPPOSITE *the first Violetta, Fanny Salvini-Donatelli, and a snatch of music from the opera that Verdi wrote in her album – her aria* 'Gran Dio morir si giovane' ('Dear God, to die so young').

LA TRAVIATA

Libretto di Francesco Maria Piave

MUSICA DI

GIUSEPPE VERDI

Ufficiale della Legion d'Onore

RIDUZIONE PER PIANOFORTE SOLO

DI

LUIGI TRUZZI e EMMANUELE MUZIO

Proprietà dell'Editore che si riserva il diritto della stampa di tutte le riduzioni e traduzioni di quest'Opera.

MILANO
REGIO STABILIMENTO NAZIONALE
TITO DI GIO. RICORDI
FIRENZE, Ricordi e Jouhaud. — MENDRISIO, Bustelli-Rossi. — PARIGI, Leone Escudier.

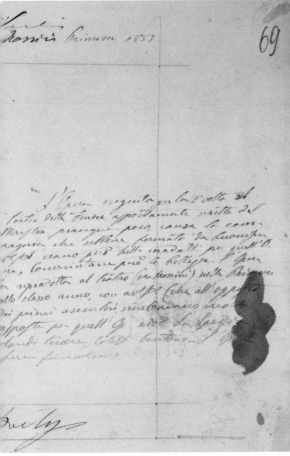

69

A

FANNY SALVINI DONATELLI

Even before *Traviata* opened Verdi dictated a letter conveying his belief that the entire company of singers was unworthy of La Fenice, and that the result would be a complete failure. He was right. Verdi wrote after the premiere: '*La Traviata* was a grand fiasco, and what is worse, they laughed. However, I'm not disturbed about it. Am I wrong, or are they wrong? I believe myself that the last word on *La Traviata* is not that of last night. They will see it again – and we shall see!'[24]

Time did of course tell: Antonio Gallo had been impresario at La Fenice for the disastrous premiere of *La Traviata* in 1853 and was determined to revive the opera in his family's theatre. Not more than fourteen months later, on 6 May 1854, *La Traviata* opened in the San Benedetto theatre to thundering applause. It was reported that 'the enthusiasm is indescribable . . . The same audience that first condemned the work now pride themselves on having known all along what a marvellous opera it always was.'[25] Was *ottocento* Venice that fickle? Perhaps it was a bad time for Venice, but better ones were on the way. When Venice was returned to Italy in 1866, the crowds weeping and cheering King Victor Emmanuel's arrival were also celebrating the conclusion of over half a century of embarrassment and shame for the once proud Serenissima.

For some, the Venetian opera *par excellence* is Ponchielli's *La Gioconda*. This, writes Julian Budden,

offers a panorama of the city in all its contrasting aspects: the Venice of perpetual carnival, of regattas and splendid ceremonies; and at the same time the sinister Venice with its State Inquisition, its notorious Council of Ten and its network of spies. Many people, beginning with Bernard Shaw, have dismissed the opera as bad Verdi, but that is like saying that Webster is bad Shakespeare. The real problem with *La Gioconda* is that it is a mightily expensive opera to mount. It needs six first-rate principals and it contains a substantial ballet.

Richard Wagner was to visit Venice several times during the last half of the 19th century. In his autobiography, *Mein Leben*, Wagner recalls his fear on encountering a gondola for the first time:

The weather had suddenly turned somewhat unpleasant, and the sight of the gondola itself had shocked me a bit; for despite all I had heard of these conveyances, painted black on black, the actual sight of one was still a rude surprise: when I had to go under the black awning, my first thought was a revival of a fear of cholera that I had previously mastered; it decidedly seemed to me as if I were taking part in a funeral procession during an epidemic.[26]

Despite this initial trepidation, Wagner found Venice exceedingly interest-ing. Like Tchaikovsky, he revelled in the quiet and stillness of the city. '. . . Venice was a happy choice . . . I am greatly attracted by the place, which is so unique and melancholy: I desire the most absolute privacy, and I can certainly find this better here than anywhere else. And so I am hoping for a calm and undisturbed frame of mind with which to resume my work.'[27]

Wagner found lodgings in the deserted Giustiniani palace on the Grand Canal. Many of the palaces in Venice were abandoned by their former aristocratic owners and converted into apartments for foreign visitors. These secluded quarters provided a conducive environment for Wagner to complete Act II of *Tristan*:

Never before have I worked so intimately; every stroke of my pen has the significance of an eternity for me: and I do not continue until I feel attracted by what I have written. It is a strange feeling to survey the thing as a whole and realize that never before have I written anything of such musical unity, of such inexhaustible fluency. *Tristan* will be beautiful!'[28]

Richard Wagner first came to Venice in September 1858 to seek peace: 'the actual stillness – one never hears a carriage – is indispensable for me . . . . I am now returning to Tristan, *that it may speak to you of the profound art of resonant silence.'*

However two things were to mar Wagner's sojourn in Venice. During this time he was plagued by ill health, suffering from dysentery and a painful ulcer on his leg. He was also plagued by the police. Venice was still under the iron rule of the Austrian Empire; as a former revolutionary Wagner found himself constantly under harassment. He noted the stifled atmosphere in this period of repression:

There was little to attract my attention in the very oppressed and degenerate life of the Venetian populace, for as far as human activity in the glorious ruins of this wonderful city was concerned, the only impression I was able to form was that it was maintained as a bathing resort for tourists . . . The bandmaster of the two Austrian regiments stationed in Venice got the idea of playing overtures of mine . . . The two bands took turns playing in the evening in the middle of a brilliantly illuminated St Mark's Square, which offered a truly superb acoustical setting for such music . . . I did not know which dazzled me most – the incomparable square in its magnificent illumination filled with countless numbers of moving people, or the music which seemed to be wafting all these phenomena aloft in a resounding transfiguration. But there was one thing utterly lacking here which one would otherwise have certainly expected from an Italian audience: thousands of people grouped themselves around the band and listened to the music with intense concentration; but no two hands ever forgot themselves to the extent of applauding, for any sign of approbation for an Austrian military band would have been looked upon as treason to the motherland . . .[29]

In the spring of 1859 Wagner left Venice; it was clearly dangerous for him to remain there any longer when a clash between Italian nationalists and the Austrian military became imminent.

Wagner returned briefly to Venice to visit friends in 1861. During this stay he saw Titian's 'Assumption of the Virgin'. In his autobiography Wagner writes that he was so awed by the masterpiece that it inspired him to begin the composition of *Die Meistersinger*.

In September 1882, Wagner moved to Venice with his wife Cosima and family. They occupied the mezzanine floor of the Palazzo Vendramin which is now next to the music conservatory. Extracts from the diary that Cosima Wagner kept tell us of what were to be Wagner's last few months: '16th September 1882; It is grey, but the city and the Palazzo Vendramin pleases . . .' '25th September 1882 . . . his pleasure in Venice and our lodging grows every day. The Palazzo opposite us has one storey just as he likes it, he loves the house and to see over the garden, the gondolas gliding along he finds charming.' '29th September 1882: he says that the Italians should be beaten alone for the reason that they abolish the drum and change to the 'vile' high trumpet. He compares the present flutes in an orchestra to the whistle of a steam boat.'[30]

When Wagner came to Venice for the last time in September 1882 he was already a sick man. On Christmas Eve he conducted his youthful Symphony in C Major as a birthday present for his wife Cosima, but a few weeks later he was dead. RIGHT portrait of Wagner made by Paul von Joukovsky on the very eve of his death, against the score of the C Major Symphony. BELOW Wagner and Cosima (she much taller than he) at the door of the Palazzo Vendramin.

Wagner had recently developed heart trouble. This did not prevent him from rehearsing a special performance of his youthful Symphony in C Major in honour of Cosima's birthday. He suffered a heart attack during the last rehearsal on 22 December; nevertheless he managed to conduct the performance for his invited guests at La Fenice on Christmas Eve.

Wagner died on the afternoon of 13 February 1883. Cosima sat all night talking to her dead husband and would not be parted from him for 25 hours. She cut off her hair, which had always been Wagner's delight and laid it on his breast. Three days later the cortège moved silently along the Grand Canal to the station and the train which would bring him slowly back to Bayreuth.

Perhaps the most eloquent tribute to Wagner's time in Venice was written by his own hand:

On a sleepless night that drove me out on the balcony of my apartment at about three o'clock in the morning, I heard for the first time the famous old folksong of the gondolieri. I thought the first call, piercing the stillness of the night like a harsh lament, emanated from the Rialto, barely a quarter hour's distance away, or thereabouts; from a similar distance this would be answered from another quarter in the same way. This strange melancholy dialogue, which was repeated frequently at longish intervals, moved me too much for me to be able to fix its musical components in my mind. Yet on another occasion I learned that this folksong had an indisputably poetic interest. When I was riding back late one evening along the dark canal, the moon came out and illuminated, together with the indescribable palaces, the tall silhouette of my gondolier towering above the stern of his gondola, while he slowly turned his mighty oar. Suddenly from his breast came a mournful sound not unlike the howl of an animal, swelling up from a deep, low note, and after a long-sustained 'Oh', it culminated in the simple musical phrase 'Venezia'. This was followed by some words I could not retain in my memory, being so greatly shaken by the emotion of the moment. Such were the impressions that seemed most characteristic of Venice to me during my stay . . .[31]

'My grand-piano, which has been held up in Zurich until now, is expected to arrive within the next day or so.' – Wagner to Hans von Bülow, 27 September 1858.

V   The Twentieth Century

*W*hen, at 9.55 in the morning of 14 July 1902, the Campanile of St Mark, having stood for only a decade short of a thousand years, subsided to the ground, it left the priceless buildings around it virtually untouched, depositing the golden angel at its summit on the front steps of the basilica and killing nobody but the custodian's cat. 'Il campanile', the Venetians agreed, 'è stato un galantuomo' – the campanile had behaved like a gentleman; 'com' erà, dov' erà' – as it was, where it was – it must be rebuilt. And so it came about that on the Feast of St Mark, 25 April 1912, precisely a millennium after the foundation of its predecessor, there was inaugurated the new tower that still stands today.

It was an inauspicious beginning; and there have been several subsequent moments during the century when many people, inside and outside the city, have wondered whether Venice herself would survive. During the First World War no less than 620 bombs were dropped on the city; one of them destroyed the Tiepolo ceiling in the church of the Scalzi, but by another near miracle relatively little other damage was done. Had Venice been selected for similar treatment during the Second, she would not have been so lucky; with the annihilation of Dresden still in our minds, we can only be thankful that Italy was no longer an enemy when the Baedeker raids began.

Oddly enough, Venice has suffered a good deal less in war than she has in peace; for it was in the inter-war period, and again in the fifties and sixties, that there sprang up just a mile or two away the vast industrial complex of Porto Marghera. In the early years this promised well; north-east Italy was economically prostrate, and the idea of siting vital new industries on the mainland, away from the historic city but within easy reach of her inhabitants, seemed ingeniously to combine the twin necessities of employment and conservation. But the decision in the fifties to build a new industrial zone, effectively trebling the old one in size while at the same time dramatically increasing the petro-chemical element, has in recent years threatened Venice with destruction. The principal problem, inevitably, has been that of atmospheric pollution, with sulphurous emissions combining with the natural humidity and salinity of the Venetian air to produce virulently corrosive fumes which attack stone, marble, brick, even bronze – in short, the entire fabric of the city. To make matters worse, the new industries sank artesian wells for their water supplies, with the result that the fresh-water table beneath the lagoon – a perfectly adequate source for a domestic population of some hundred thousand, but hopelessly inadequate for the needs of modern technology – began to decrease alarmingly, with a corresponding effect on subsidence. By the mid-1960s, parts of the city were sinking ten times as fast as they had been forty years before.

Such was the situation when, on 4–5 November 1966, Venice suffered the most disastrous floods in her history: the waters rose more than six feet above mean sea level and whole districts were submerged — and not only in water, but in every sort of detritus: garbage, sewage and — most damaging of all — fuel oil. Suddenly, the world woke up to the realization that its most beautiful city was in serious danger; the Italian Government, recognizing that the problem was not one that any nation could tackle single-handed, wisely referred it to UNESCO, which commissioned a technical report and appealed to its members for help; and those members launched the biggest, most ambitious and most exciting international artistic and architectural conservation project that the world has ever seen. A quarter of a century later, work still continues; and though Venice's troubles are by no means over, the dreadful triple menace of rising sea, sinking land and polluted air is now rapidly diminishing. Unfortunately, as it does so, a new danger grows: the uncontrolled spread of tourism, which threatens to make the city uninhabitable. How this problem will be met, heaven only knows; but if action is not taken soon it may well prove the most destructive of all.

Visitors who spend a night or more in the city are as welcome as they have always been; but in recent years there has emerged a new phenomenon: the hordes of day tourists — some forty to fifty thousand a day in the summer months, and on peak days twice that number — who arrive in the morning and leave the same evening, who bring packed lunches, spend practically nothing and — since the large majority never wander more than a couple of hundred yards from St Mark's and the Doge's Palace — are literally wearing the centre of the city away. Not only do they destroy the whole atmosphere of the Piazza, to the point where it looks less like Napoleon's plus beau salon de l'Europe than a large department store two shopping days before Christmas; they make life increasingly unpleasant for the working population of the city, which has declined from 100,000 to 85,000 in the past quarter of a century.

It seems, therefore, all too clear that Venice's primary need today is a dramatic reduction in their numbers; she will then have to attract back her former inhabitants by building plenty of good, low-cost housing and finally by introducing new industries unconnected with the tourist trade. How the first of these ends is to be achieved heaven only knows (not, certainly, by means of the so-called Expo 2000, enthusiastically championed by Italy's Foreign Minister in 1989–90, which, had the proposal not been withdrawn at the last moment, would have celebrated the turn of the century by bringing in 30 million additional visitors over a period of four months); but the other two are perfectly possible, owing to the number of abandoned islands in the lagoon which could easily be reclaimed without damaging the historic city. Two of these islands, S. Giorgio Maggiore and S. Servolo, have already provided perfect examples of what can be done: the first with its world-famous Cini Foundation, the second with its superb school of advanced craftsmanship, running under the auspices of the Council of Europe and attended by students from all over the continent and beyond.

Venice, in short, remains in peril. Obliged as she has always been to maintain that vital equilibrium of land and water to which she owes her existence, she must now struggle to keep the balance between beauty and practicality, between her historic character and the demands of modern life, between the conflicting interests of her domestic population and the package tour. Other cities, to be sure, have similar problems; but Venice is not like other cities. She is more delicate than they, and infinitely more fragile. If, over the next crucial decade, she surmounts her difficulties, there is no reason why she should not enter the third millennium with confidence and hope. If she fails, she will collapse — just as surely and just as completely as the campanile of St Mark collapsed, that summer morning nearly a century ago.

The new century arrived in Venice literally with a big bang. The magnificent campanile of San Marco collapsed in 1902 – as if the decline of the great city was being spelled out. But the authorities set to work at once to rebuild it, and on St Mark's Day, 25 April 1912, the newly reconstructed bell tower was inaugurated in a lofty ceremony. The number of people wanting to share in this great symbolic gesture was so large that tickets had to be issued – Venice will not die and the proud tower was there to bear witness to the fact.

One of the visitors was the American art-historian Bernard Berenson, who had first come to Venice as a young man in October 1888 and was immediately enchanted by the lagoon city. He was sure it would haunt him 'for ever and ever',[1] indeed he returned there throughout his life.

At 10 o'clock in the morning of 14 July 1902, the Campanile of San Marco, the most conspicuous landmark in Venice, suddenly collapsed without warning. Miraculously, it subsided into itself, leaving San Marco untouched and only slightly damaging the Library on the other side. But the heap of rubble filled half the piazza.

Two world wars left Venice virtually unscathed, though a stray bomb in 1915 destroyed Tiepolo's ceiling in the church of the Scalzi. This photograph shows the courtyard of the Ducal Palace and the Scala dei Giganti protected by sandbags in World War I.

In this soul-stirring ceremony of 1912, brilliant banners hung from the pillars; they hauled up the battle flag of the cruiser *San Marco* to the top of the campanile; a huge cannon boomed and all the bells began to sound. A trumpet call sounded: massed children's choirs began to sing the old 'Cantata del Campanile'. Two thousand carrier pigeons were released and carried the message of the rebuilt campanile to the whole of Italy. The carabinieri with their scarlet and blue plumes escorted the bishops and other high dignitaries of the church, leaving the basilica for the platform facing the Duke of Genoa and the ceremony of consecration began. Berenson recalled, 'I began to sob and blubber and choke'.[2]

The 20th century saw Venice becoming ever more of a museum. The number of tourists increased rapidly when it was easier to reach the island city without the necessity of using a boat and of course direct access by railway had already made Venice easily approachable from Continental Europe. As the hordes of tourists increased, indigenous life changed rapidly. The spring, summer and autumn months became more and more a tourist industry for the local population. But musical life suffered. As opera declined in Italy, many of the theatres in Venice were totally transformed: The 'Malibran' and 'Rossini' Theatres became cinemas, others were closed. Only the famous Teatro La Fenice and the Teatro Goldoni continued to function, the former for opera and the latter for comedy, with seasons of mediocre calibre. In 1947 the Teatro Goldoni was closed for security reasons.

In 1930, however, there was a dramatic change. A Festival of theatre, music and cinema was soon turned into the world-famous 'Biennale di Venezia', which soon brought crowds of celebrities to Venice as well as a desperately needed injection of vital culture from outside. To a certain extent, the Biennale took place outside the city's cultural life, at the palazzo Grassi and the Fondazione Cini on the island of San Giorgio, attracting more crowds from outside than local inhabitants. The situation was not unlike that of Salzburg, where Mozart's birthplace became transformed for five weeks round August every year into a great international music centre, after which time Salzburg slipped quickly back to its sleepy, small-town way of life.

During World War II, of course, the Biennale lapsed, but as soon as hostilities had ceased, the authorities wanted to revive it. In 1948, the director of the Tate Gallery told Bernard Berenson that the British Council had voted 'to show our greatest master, Turner, together with our most widely admired modern master, Henry Moore'. Berenson had a fit. 'The two most destructive personalities in European art today . . . are Picasso and Moore', said the conservative American art-historian whose scientific approach to Renaissance painting had revolutionized art history. 'Picasso [is] consciously destructive, and Moore unconsciously . . . If Picasso and Moore are meaningful, then the Egyptians, the Greeks, the Florentines, the Venetians, the Netherlanders are not.' Contemporary sculptures and paintings at the Biennale exhibition, said Berenson, did not 'come at all under the category of art'. They interested him none the less 'by their impudence, their absurdity, their unconsciousness.'[3]

The wealthy American art patroness Peggy Guggenheim bought an unfinished palazzo on the Grand Canal. Berenson went there and asked her, looking about at her modern sculptures, 'Why do you go in for this?' Peggy Guggenheim archly said she couldn't afford Old Masters and she also considered it her duty to 'protect the art of one's time'. Berenson, who had made a speciality of discovering and identifying old masters in remote churches in Umbria and Tuscany and then selling them to rich American collectors like Isabella Gardiner for a fortune, turned to Peggy Guggenheim and said, 'You should have come to me, my dear, I would have found you bargains'.[4]

*   *   *

The outside theatre, Teatro Verde (Green Theatre), was inaugurated in 1954 and gave a whole series of successful performances. Perhaps the most important theatrical event in post-war Venice was the inauguration of an International Festival of Contemporary Music, which yielded several pieces of scandal or fame or both: in 1959 *Il Circo Maz* by G. Negri, *Diagramma circolare* by A. Bruni-Tedeschi and *Allez-hop* by Luciano Berio, and in 1962 the scandalous opera, which was almost hissed off the boards, Luigi Nono's *Intolleranza 1960*, wherein Bruno Maderna the conductor persevered in salvaging the music when it was thought that the opera would have to stop completely.

Certainly the most important and far-reaching musical event for 20th-century Venice was Igor Stravinsky's love for the city and his decision to launch there his celebrated opera *The Rake's Progress*. It came about in a curious fashion. In May 1947 there was an exhibition in Chicago of the British painter William Hogarth,

Serge Diaghilev first came to Venice at the age of eighteen and returned to it whenever he could. It was here that he died, in August 1929, and was buried on the cemetery island of S. Michele. This sketch was made by Stravinsky in 1921.

A mosaic of personalities and events that have helped to make Venice world famous as a centre of 20th-century music.
TOP *Luigi Nono with a scene from* Intolleranza 60, *which raised a storm of protest at the International Festival of Contemporary Music in 1962.*
BELOW *Luciano Berio and his wife, the singer Cathy Berberian; Berio's* Allez Hop *in 1959 found the public equally unprepared for novelty.*

whose cruel satires of British life had fascinated and repelled people for two hundred years. Stravinsky saw engravings of the cycle 'The Rake's Progress' and decided that the subject would make an excellent opera. In November 1947 the composer spent a week with his librettist, British poet, W.H. Auden, who had been teaching at Swarthmore College during and after the Second World War. Auden took as a collaborator for the libretto his friend Chester Kallman, and they were ideal partners for Stravinksy, making any small changes in the text that he required.

The message of the Hogarth prints seems to have dictated to Stravinksy the old-fashioned idea of a 'number' opera with spoken dialogue and set pieces in the manner of a Mozart opera. Stressing the symbolic and moral aspect of the tale, the composer wrote to Auden, 'I think the hero's end in an asylum scratching a fiddle would make a meritorious conclusion to his stormy life.' Soon Stravinsky was thinking directly of Mozart (always a hero to Auden too) and asking his British publishers for scores of four Mozart operas to study. There are hints of *Don Giovanni* in *The Rake's Progress* (the graveyard scene) but there is even more of the 20th century's great Mozartian discovery, *Così fan tutte*, with its terrible tale of fidelity betrayed.

The premiere of *The Rake's Progress* took place in the Teatro La Fenice in Venice on 11 September 1951 and marked the high point, and almost precisely

the mid-century celebration, of musical life in 20th-century Venice.

Stravinsky's attachment to Venice manifested itself in other compositions, too. There was the *Canticum sacrum ad honorem Sancti Marci Nominis* for tenor, baritone, chorus and orchestra, based on Vulgate texts, first given in Venice on 13 September 1956 — and a darkly magnificent tribute to one of the most haunting churches in Christendom.

This moving *Canticum sacrum* was followed, in Stravinsky's oeuvre for Venice, by *Threni: id est Lamentationes Jeremiae Prophetae* (based on the Vulgate texts of the lamentations of the Prophet Jeremiah) and first performed in Venice on 23 September 1958.

Stravinsky's pupil, Robert Craft, had been instrumental in performing and recording the extraordinary tortured music of Gesualdo, prince, murderer and composer. Stravinsky became very interested in this forward-looking master and for his anniversary wrote a *Monumentum pro Gesualdo di Venosa (ad CD Annum)*, which he caused to be first given in Venice on 27 September 1960.

Venice looked on the great Russian composer as an adopted son, and when Igor Stravinsky died in 1971 and chose to be buried in Venice, the city gave him a moving and magnificent funeral.

*   *   *

Three more controversial musical events staged at the Venice Festival.
TOP CENTRE *Diagramma circolare by A. Bruni-Tedeschi (1959).* TOP RIGHT *Circo Max by G. Negri (1959).* BOTTOM LEFT *Hyperion by Bruno Maderna (1964).* RIGHT *poster for the 1980 Biennale, with the winged lion of St. Mark howling at the moon like a giant spectral cat.*

Igor Stravinsky (RIGHT) *was as devoted to Venice as his compatriot Diaghilev, and chose La Fenice for the première of his opera* The Rake's Progress *in 1951, an event eagerly awaited by the whole musical world.* LEFT *the set for Act I, the programme, and Stravinsky at the conductor's rostrum.*

Several other works by Stravinsky were given their first performances in Venice, and when he died in 1971 his will dictated that he should be buried there next to Diaghilev. The funeral was a ceremony and a spectacle such as only Venice can bring off. Here (BELOW) *the coffin leaves the church of SS. Giovanni e Paolo.*

The German writer Thomas Mann wrote a celebrated short story, 'Death in Venice' which became even more famous when it was turned into a film by Luchino Visconti in 1962, with the hero thinly disguised as Gustav Mahler. Mahler was a great influence on the next musical tribute that Venice could celebrate. This time the composer was Benjamin Britten, who set *Death in Venice* to music; it was first performed on the stage of the Maltings, Aldeburgh, on 16 June 1973, then at Covent Garden to honour the composer's birthday on 22 November, St Cecilia's Day. Britten tried to capture the mood of the enigmatic short story. Mann himself wrote to his children in May 1932: 'In spirit I am with you leading that unique life between the warm sea in the morning and the "ambiguous" city in the afternoon. Ambiguous . . . is wonderfully relevant in all its meanings, and for all the city's modern silliness and corruptness . . . this musical magic of ambiguity still lives . . . For certain people, there is a special melancholia associated with the name of Venice . . .'[5]

And there is the sea – so much a part of Britten's operatic triumphs. The sea is omnipresent in *Death in Venice* too, as when Aschenbach approaches Venice by boat, and especially after the hotel manager has shown Aschenbach his room and the visitor looks at the sea from his hotel window.

*   *   *

Gian Francesco Malipiero came from an old and distinguished Venetian family. He lived to a grand old age, dying at the age of ninety-one, the very year of Britten's *Death in Venice* – 1973.

Malipiero will probably not go down in history as a great composer – his operas with their echoes of 18th-century Venice such as the *Commedie goldoniane*, written in 1926, are already nearly forgotten and even his pretty orchestral music, like the *Serenissima*, is hardly played outside Italy. But Malipiero will certainly be remembered for his great and generous act in printing and editing the first complete edition of the music of Claudio Monteverdi, often doing the actual transcribing himself. Not content with that, Malipiero was closely connected with the great Vivaldi revival that coincided with the outbreak of World War II. He edited many of the great Vivaldi concertos – opus 3 (*L'estro armonico*), opus 8 (*Il cimento dell'armonia e dell'inventione*), which of course opens with the most famous popular piece of classical music in the world, *The Four Seasons*, and opus 9, (*La cetra [The lyre]*). Malipiero rendered an immortal service to Italian music of the 17th and 18th centuries and was an honour and credit to his great native city.

But Venice, as everyone knows, has many problems, not only ecological but also internal. Many international organizations are dedicated to trying to save the Serenissima from total collapse – not least the Venice in Peril Fund, headed by Sir Ashley Clark. But the prognoses are indeed dire, and one hundred years from now, many of the beautiful images seen in this book will no longer exist.

49　The picturesque *Rio di S. Trovaso connects the Grand Canal with the Giudecca Canal. It has one of Venice's few surviving boat yards where traditional techniques going back for centuries are still practised.*

Notes

I THE GABRIELIS AND THE SIXTEENTH CENTURY

1. John Julius Norwich, *Venice: The Greatness and the Fall*, London 1979, p.198f.
2. Quoted by James Cleugh, *The Divine Aretino: Pietro of Arezzo 1592–1556*, London 1965.
3. Hugh Honour, *The Companion Guide to Venice*, London 1965, p.23.
4. Sir Richard Torkington, *The Oldest Diary of English Travel*, London 1883.
5. R. Lassels, *The Voyage of Italy*, Paris 1670.
6. F. Sansovina, *Venetia Città Nobilissima*, Venice 1604 and 1663 editions.
7. Logan Pearsall, *The Life and Letters of Sir Henry Wotton*, Oxford 1907.
8. Thomas Coryat, *Coryat's Crudities Hastily Gobled Up in Five Months' Travel*, London 1611.
9. An example of extra musicians being hired is given in the St Mark's accounts for 21 April 1568, when the treasury paid eight scudi for the hire of four muted cornets, two alto cornets, a *cornamusa* (bagpipes) and a *piffero* (flute) to play in the organ loft on a festival day.
10. Denis Arnold, *Giovanni Gabrieli and The Music of the Venetian High Renaissance*, Oxford 1979, p.8.
11. Denis Arnold, p.9.
12. Quoted in Denis Arnold, p.17.

II MONTEVERDI AND THE SEVENTEENTH CENTURY

1. Quoted in John Julius Norwich: *Venice: The Greatness And The Fall*, London 1981, p.255.
2. Thomas Nashe, *The Unfortunate Traveller*, London 1594.
3. John Evelyn, *The Diary*, London 1905.
4. Quoted in Denis Arnold, *Monteverdi*, London 1963, p.26.
5. Quoted in Denis Arnold, p.15.
6. Quoted in Denis Arnold, p.13.
7. H.E. Redlich, *Claudio Monteverdi: Life and Works*, Oxford 1952, p.94.
8. Quoted in Denis Arnold, p.16.
9. Quoted in Denis Arnold, p.21.
10. Quoted in H.E. Redlich, p.19f.
11. Quoted in Denis Arnold, p.30.
12. Quoted in H.E. Redlich, p.28.
13. Quoted in H.E. Redlich, p.34.
14. Denis Stevens, *The Letters of Claudio Monteverdi*, London 1980, p.419.
15. Obituary written by Camberlotti, quoted in Denis Arnold, p.47.
16. Quoted in H.J. Moser, *Heinrich Schütz: Sein Leben und Werk*, Germany 1954, p.114f.
17. Quoted in H.J. Moser, p.46.
18. Quoted in H.J. Moser, p. 115.
19. Quoted in H.J. Moser, p.115.
20. Quoted in H.J. Moser, p.115.
21. Quoted in H.J. Moser, p.116.
22. Jane Glover, *Cavalli*, London 1978.
23. Ellen Rosand, 'The Voice of Barbara Strozzi' in *Women Making Music* (ed. Jane Bowers and Judith Tick), University of Illinois Press, pp.168–189.

III VIVALDI AND THE EIGHTEENTH CENTURY

1. Christopher Hibbert, *The Grand Tour*, London 1987, p.128.
2. Joseph Addison, *Remarks on Several Parts of Italy 1701–1703*, London 1705.
3. Mary Wortley Montague, *The Letters and Works of Lady Mary Wortley Montague*, London 1887.
4. John Julius Norwich, *Venice: the Greatness and the Fall*, London 1981, p.335f.
5. Joseph Addison, op. cit.
6. Joseph Addison, op. cit.
7. J.B.S. Morritt, *A Grand Tour: Letters and Journeys 1794–96*, London 1985, p.304f.
8. Quoted in Christopher Hibbert, *The Grand Tour*, London 1987, p.133.
9. John Moore, *A View of Society and Manners in Italy*, Dublin 1792, 3 vols, vol 1 p.41f.
10. J.B.S. Morritt, p.305.
11. F. Stefani, *Sei Lettre di Antonio Vivaldi veneziano, maestro compositione di musica della prima meta del secolo XVIII*, Venice 1871.
12. Carlo Goldoni, *Memoirs of Goldoni Written By Himself*, translated by John Black, London 1814.
13. E. Wright, *Some Observations Made in Travelling Through France, Italy etc In the Years 1720, 1721 and 1722*, London 1730, 2 vols, vol 1 p.79.
14. J.J. Rousseau, *Confessions*, Part II Book 7.
15. P. Molmenti, *Venezia nella vita privata*, London 1906–8, 4 vols.
16. Vivaldi literature is vast. Two recent books may be cited: Michael Talbot, *Vivaldi*, London 1978, and Alan Kendall, *Vivaldi*, London 1978.
17. John Mainwaring, *Memoirs of the Life of the late George Frederic Handel*, London 1760, p.51f.

IV GRAND OPERA AND THE NINETEENTH CENTURY

1. Benjamin Disraeli, *Contarini Fleming: A Psychological Romance*, London 1832.
2. Quoted in James Morris, *The World of Venice*, Pantheon Books, NY, 1960, p.118.
3. William Wordsworth, 'On the Extinction of the Venetian Republic' (1802).
4. *The Diary of Lady Frances Shelley, 1789–1817*, ed. R. Edgcumbe, NY, 1912, p.330–31.
5. George Gordon Lord Byron, *Childe Harold*, Canto IV.
6. Percy Bysshe Shelley, *The Letters*, ed. Frederick L. Jones,

Oxford 1964.

7. ibid., p.334–35.

8. William Weaver, *The Golden Century of Italian Opera, from Rossini to Puccini*, London 1980, p.7.

9. *The Musical Journeys of Louis Spohr*, ed. Henry Pleasant, Oklahoma Press 1961, p.151.

10. ibid., p. 154–55.

11. Felix Mendelssohn, *Letters*, London 1877 (Letter to an old professor).

12. Quoted in George Macaulay Trevelyan, *Manin and the Venetian Revolution of 1848*, London 1923.

13. William Dean Howells, *Venetian Life*, Boston 1867.

14. Mark Twain, *The Innocents Abroad*, NY, 1869, p.217.

15. Henry James, 'Venice: An Early Impression' [essay] 1872.

16. Francis Toye, *A Study in Tragi-Comedy*, London 1954, p.19.

17. ibid., p.31.

18. Frank Walker, *The Man Verdi*, London 1962, p.147.

19. ibid. (Letter from Emanuele Muzio to Barezzi; 23 March 1846).

20. Weaver op. cit. p.145–46. (Letter to Francesco Maria Piave; 28 April 1850).

21. Carlo Gatti, *Verdi*, Milano, Vol I 1931, p.353.

22. Weaver op. cit. p.146–48.

23. Gatti op. cit. p.358.

24. Walker op. cit. p.296.

25 Carteggi, *Verdiani I*, ed. A. Luzio, Rome 1935, p.24.

26 Richard Wagner, *My Life*, London, (1988 ed), p.572.

27. *Selected Letters of Richard Wagner*, translated and edited by Stewart Spencer and Barry Millington, London 1987, 420. (Letter to Hans Bülow; 27 September 1858.)

28. ibid., 448. (Letter to Eliza Wille; 21 February 1859.)

29. Wagner, op. cit.,

30. Cosima Wagner, *Die Tagebucher 1878–1883* Vol II, Munchen 1977, pp. 1003–9.

31. Wagner, op. cit.

V CONTEMPORARY MUSIC AND THE TWENTIETH CENTURY

1. Ernest Samuels, *Bernard Berenson The Making of a Legend*, Cambridge, Massachusetts, 1987, p.141.

2. ibid. p.142.

3. ibid. p.521.

4. ibid.

5. *The British Companion*, ed. Christopher Palmer, London 1984, p.251.

Suggested Listening: A Discography

Sarah Bonner-Morgan

PALESTRINA, Giovanni Pierluigi di (1525–94)

Missa Papae Marcelli
    Westminster Cathedral Choir; Hill
    Hyperion CDA 66266

LASSUS, Orlandus (c.1530–94)

Motets & Chansons
    Hilliard Ensemble, Hillier
    EMI CD C7 49210–2

GABRIELI, Andrea (1515–1586)

"A Venetian Coronation" 1595
    (incl. music by G. Gabrieli/Bendinelli)
    Gabrieli Consort & Players, McCreesh
    Virgin VCT 791110

GABRIELI, Giovanni (1557–1612)

Canzoni da Sonare
    Hesperion XX
    EMI Reflexe CDM 7631412

SCHÜTZ, Heinrich (1585–1672)

Symphoniae Sacrae op.6
    Les Saqueboutiers de Toulouse
    Erato ECD 88150
"Christmas Story"
    (incl. G. Gabrieli *Four Christmas Motets*)
    Kings Consort, Robert King
    Hyperion CDA 66398
Italian Madrigals (Book 1 Complete)
    Consort of Musicke, Rooley
    EMI CDC7 47600–2

MONTEVERDI, Claudio (1567–1643)

Sacred Vocal Music
    Kirkby, Partridge, Thomas, Parley of Instruments
    Hyperion CDA 66021
Madrigals (Books 4 & 6)
    Consort of Musicke, Rooley
    Decca O/L 414 148–2 410 291–2
Vespro della Beata Vergine (Vespers)
    English Baroque Soloists, Monteverdi Choir, Gardiner
    DG Archiv 429 565–2
"L'Orfeo" – (Favola in Musica)
    Rolfe-Johnson, Baird, Dawson, Von Otter
    Argenta, Robson, Monteverdi Choir,
    English Baroque Soloists, Gardiner
    DG Archiv 419 250–2
"L'incoronazione di Poppea"
    Donath, Soderstrom, Berberian,
    Esswood, Luccardi, Gartner, Gaifa, Hansmann,
    Langridge, Equiluz.

    Vienna Concentus Musicus, Harnoncourt
    Teldec ZC8 35247
"L'incoronazione di Poppea"
    Auger, Jones, Hirst, Bowman, Leonard, Reinhart,
    Thomson.
    City of London Sinfonia, Hickox
    Virgin VCT 790775
Lamento d'Arianna
    Cathy Berberian
    Vienna Concentus Musicus, Harnoncourt
    Teldec ZS8 43635

CAVALLI, (Pietro) Francesco (1602–1676)

"Xerse"
    R. Jacobs, Nelson, Gall, Poulenard, Mellon, Feldman,
    Elwes, De Mey, Visse
    Instrumental Ensemble, Jacobs
    Harmonia Mundi HMC 901175/8

STROZZI, Barbara (1619–?)

Solo vocal music
    Glenda Simpson
    Camerata of London
    Hyperion CDA 66303

VIVALDI, Antonio (1675–1741)

"L'Estro Armonico" (12 Concertos) op.3
    Holloway, Huggett, Mackintosh, Wilcock,
    Academy of Ancient Music, Hogwood
    Decca O/L 414 554–2
"La Stravaganza" (12 Violin Concertos) op.4
    Huggett, Academy of Ancient Music, Hogwood
    Decca O/L 417 502–2
6 Flute Concertos, op.10
    Lisa Beznosiuk, English Concert, Pinnock
    DG Archiv 423 702–2
Vivaldi/Albinoni Wind Concertos
    Kings Consort, King
    Hyperion CDA 66383
Trio Sonatas (various)
    Purcell Quartet
    Hyperion CDA 66193
Cello Sonatas (1–6)
    Christophe Coin
    Hogwood, Zweistra, Ferre, Finucane
    Decca O/L 421 060–2
Nisi Dominus (Psalm 126) RV608
Stabat Mater RV621
    Bowman, Academy of Ancient Music, Hogwood
    Decca O/L 414 329–2
Gloria in D RV589
    Argenta, Attrot, Denley,
    English Concert, Pinnock
    DG Archiv 423 386–2

"Orlando Furioso"
Horne, De los Angeles, Valentini, Tervani, Gonzales,
Kozman, Bruscantini, Zaccaria,
Solisti Veneti, Scimone
Erato ECD 88190
"L'Incoronazione di Dario"
Elwes, Lesne, Ledroit, Verschaere, Poulenard, Mellon,
Visse
Nice Baroque Ensemble, Bezzina
Harmonia Mundi HMC 901235/7
The Four Seasons (from op.8)
Standage, English Concert, Pinnock
DG Archiv 400 045-2
Kennedy, English Chamber Orchestra
EMI CDC7 49557-2
Ayo, I Musici
Philips 422139-2

BACH, Johann Sebastian (1685–1750)

4-Harpsichord Concerto
Pinnock, Gilbert, Mortensen, Kraemer
English Concert
DG Archiv 400041-2

HANDEL, George Frederick (1685–1759)

Overtures (incl. Sinfonia to Agrippina)
English Concert, Pinnock
DG Archiv 419 219-2
Opera Arias (incl. Agrippina : Bel Piacere)
Marilyn Horne, Solisti Veneti, Scimone
Erato ECD 88034

ROSSINI, Gioacchino (1792–1868)

*Overtures (incl. La Cambiale, L'Inganno Felice, L'Italiana, La Scala
di Seta, Tancredi)*
Orpheus Chamber Orchestra
DG 415 363-2
"L'Italiana in Algeri"
Baltsa, Raimondi, Dora, Lopardo
Vienna State Opera Chorus, Vienna Philharmonic
Orchestra, Abbado
DG 427 331-2
"Tancredi"
Horne, Cuberli, Palacio, Zaccaria, Di Nissa, Schuman
La Fenice Chorus & Orchestra, Weikert
CBS M3K 39073
Arias (Various)
Marilyn Horne, Ambrosian Opera Chorus
Royal Philharmonic Orchestra, Lewis
Decca 421 306-2

VERDI, Giuseppe (1813–1901)

"Attila"
Ramey, Studer, Shicoff, Zancanaro
La Scala Milan Orchestra & Chorus, Muti
EMI CDS7 49952-2
"Ernani"
Domingo, Bruson, Ghiaurov, Freni
La Scala Milan Orchestra & Chorus, Muti
EMI CDS7 47083-8

"La Traviata"
Sutherland, Pavarotti, Manuguerra
London Opera Chorus, National P.O. Bonynge
Decca 410 154-2
"La Traviata"
Scotto, Kraus, Bruson, Buchan
Ambrosian Opera Chorus, Philharmonia Orchestra, Muti
EMI CDS7 47538-9
"Rigoletto"
Bruson, Gruberova, Shicoff, Fassbaender, Lloyd
Acc. St Cecilia Orchestra & Chorus Sinopoli
Philips 412592-2
"Rigoletto"
Gobbi, Callas, Di Stefano, Zaccaria
La Scala Milan Orchestra & Chorus, Serafin.
EMI (mono) CDS7 47469-8

WAGNER, Richard (1813–83)

"Tristan und Isolde"
Vickers, Dernesch, Ludwig, Berry, Ridderbusch, German
Opera Berlin Chorus
Berlin Philharmonic Orchestra, Karajan
EMI CMS7 693 19-2
"Tristan und Isolde"
Windgassen, Nilsson
Ludwig, Talvela, Waechter
Bayreuth Festival (1966) Chorus & Orchestra, Boehm
DG 419 889-2
"Die Meistersinger von Nurnberg"
Fischer-Dieskau, Ligendza, Lagger, Hermann, Domingo,
Laubenthal, Ludwig
German Opera Berlin Chorus & Orchestra, Jochum
DG 415 278-2

STRAVINSKY, Igor Feodorovich (1882–1971)

"The Rake's Progress"
Langridge, Pope, Walker, Ramey, Dean, Dobson
London Sinfonietta Chorus & Orchestra, Chailly
Decca 411 644-2

BRITTEN, Benjamin (1913–77)

"Death in Venice"
Pears, Shirley-Quirk, Bowman, Bowen, Leeming,
Williams, Mackay, Sanders
English Opera Group, English Chamber Orchestra,
Bedford
Decca 425669-2

MADERNA, Bruno (1920–1973)

"Quadrivium", "Aura"
North German Radio Symphony Orchestra
DG 423246-2

NONO, Luigi (1924–1990)

"Liebeslied"
Vienna Youth Choir, Vienna Philharmonic, Abbado
DG 429260-2

"SOUVENIRS DE VENISE"
Rolfe-Johnson, Songmakers' Almanac
Hyperion CDA 66112

Sources of Illustrations

Index